Summary Aide Memoire

There are many acronyms, processes, standards and procedures in organized and operational groups.

The Emergency Response Team Search and Rescue (ERTSAR) is no different. We have established standards, best practices, processes and methods in this document presented as an "Aide Memoire."

For the most part the following document is a reminder and guidance to the standards and methods.

It usually will require the training that goes with it to provide context and substance.

Some of this is also referenced in other documents like the Marine Unit SOPs and Documents.

CERTIFICATION RECORD

This page is to note any and all training and certificates you hold and note their expiry as well as recertification. Tech Rescue is valid for 2 years.

It is a requirement that all members should be familiar with the SOP Manual and other supporting documents such as the Marine Unit manual for the Marine Unit etc. Seniors should have also had their LTC (Leadership Training Course – 2 days) or LTC – Lite (4-hour short intro version.)

Newer items such as the **St Mikes Award** *(Rescue & Fitness Award)* for high performing members will be referenced in notices and document sessions.

The Annual **Certificate of Competence** (formerly Primary, Secondary and Tertiary Member Rating) is required by ALL Members to pass and be operational as well as earn various specialist privileges on record.

Any Members on a LOA (Leave of Absence) will not be Operational during that time.

Also note that not everything on the ERTSAR member TEAMAPP can be seen or accessed and if you think you should be able to see more protected pages ask for access for your group. It may be denied or you may be invited to other groups and squads etc.

When signing up online please say **YES or NO** (and avoid saying Maybe). We need to plan for numbers and commitments with rosters etc.

ERTSAR uses online courses, e-Learning, Distance e-Learning (DeL) and Blended Learning etc.

We expect to be doing this more and more in future to support the essential face to face in person practical sessions when members meet and train together.

Contents

DID YOU KNOW? ... "ST3s are Full SAR TECHS!"

Did you know that the highest level of a (full) Search and Rescue Technician in ERTSAR is known as an ST3, which is the short form "Search and Rescue Technician – Level 3."

An reminder is that SAR TECHS are very highly trained rescuers and medics with practical experience and capable of operating in all areas of operations. The Level 3 is the fully trained and qualified SAR TECH within ERTSAR.

- ST1 or SAR TECH Level 1 | Is a Full Rescue Tech and Basic Medic and in the process
- ST2 or SAR TECH Level 2 | Is a qualified SAR Tech getting full experience and seniority
- ST3 or SAR TECH Level 3 | Is a fully qualified SAR TECH and able to operate & supervise

---

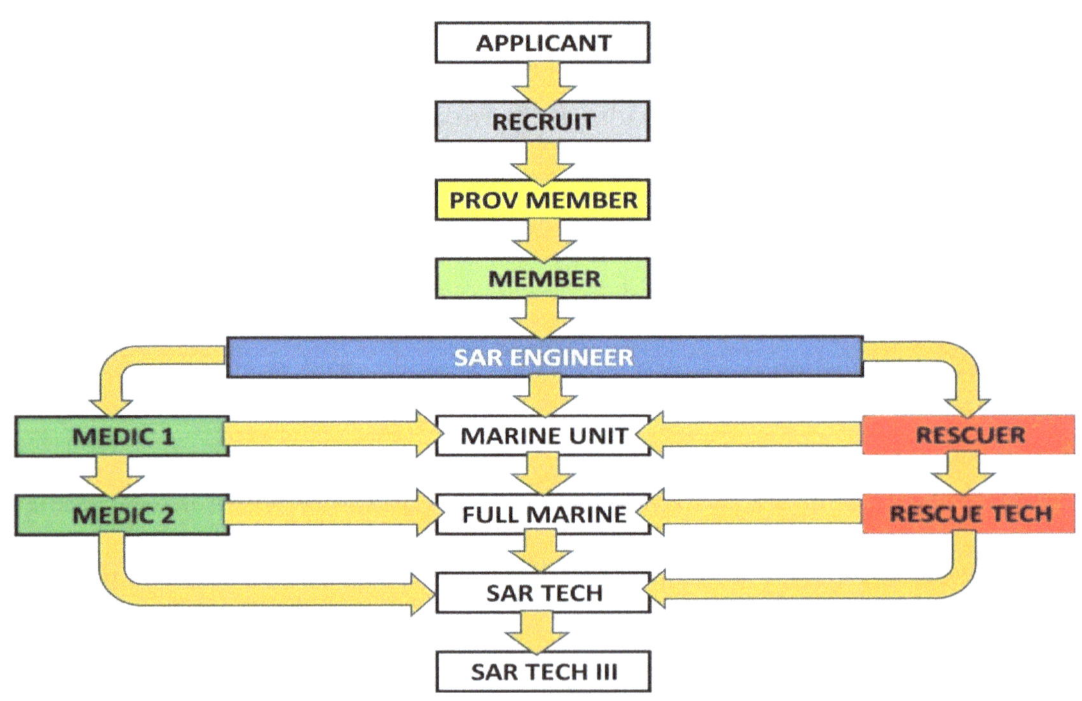

SURVIVAL

PLAN-M (This is a well-known survival mnemonic)

This helps to remind the priorities and necessities for survival especially in a rural or wilderness environment.

Protection:

- Clothing (wicking, warmth, weatherproof) and improvised clothing
- Fire building and lighting, reflectors (feather sticks, birch bark, lens, flint etc)
- Expedient shelters
- Robust shelters
- Snow survival shelters

Location:

- See and be seen (or not be seen, depending on where you are)
- Safety of location in regard to environment
- Signs to affect a rescue (use of 'magnets')
- Signal fires and signaling for rescue.

Acquisition:

- Water (purification, sources, animals as signs of water)
- Food (hunting small game, cooking, plants, food safety test)
- Surviving Resources (Medical / Health, Dry fuel for fire, shelter items, etc)

Navigation:

- Natural and improvised navigation.
- Map and compass.
- Estimating and tracking distance.

Medical:

- Foo's top 10 medical needs in an austere environment.
- Hypothermia signs and combating them.
- Improvised splints, braces, stretchers, etc.
- Natural medicines and resources.
- Management of injuries and conditions

STOPP

Remember to take a pause and think before responding to any such situation especially in an austere and remote environment.

- **S**   Stay / Stop
- **T**   Think
- **O**   Observe
- **P**   Prepare / Plan
- **P**   Proceed

Survival law of threes

This is a muddied version of the Famous law of threes

- **3 minutes without air**
- 3 minutes catastrophic bleeding
- 3 hours without shelter (harsh environment)
- **3 days without water**
- **3 weeks without food**
- 3 months without contact

12 "Cs" of Essential Kit

This is influenced from a modified version of *Dave Canterbury's* 10-piece kit, revolving around his 5 Cs of survival: Cutting tool, Covering device, Combustion device, Container made of metal, and Cordage. There are MANY out there. This is a sample list

1. **C**utting tool (i.e.metal knife, blade, scissors)
2. **C**overing device (Tent cover, Tarp, Sheets, etc)
3. **C**ombustion device *(Fire starters)*
4. **C**ontainer (Often made of metal)
5. **C**ordage. (i.e., 550 Paracord, Rope, Twine,)
6. **C**onnection & Cement (Cable ties, glue, clamps)
7. **C**argo day pack (Knapsack or rucksack, bag)
8. **C**ompass (GPS / Sat Nav / Maps etc.)
9. **C**andle-watts (Lights, Flashlights, Torches)
10. **C**ombo tool (Multi tool, folding saw, etc.)
11. **C**loth 3'x3' (i.e., Bandanna. Microfibre towel)
12. **C**ommunication Whistles, Radio, Flares,

Collective Mission Profile Items:

Traditionally different groups pack for different purposes and ERT SAR is no different.
- A team going to Artic Circle? Very warm clothing
- Military going to war? Maybe extra guns and ammo.
- Rescue team going to a medical hot climate: Rehydration salts and wicking materials. (Did you know you can wear long sleeve wicking shirts and 'summer long johns' to keep cool and mainly reduce getting bitten by bugs! **Remember to pack for the 'mission!'**

HOTZONE KIT & EQUIPMENT

Also remember that the closer we get to the action, the less kit you may be able to carry and the leaner your "load out" will have to be. Here is a graphic to visualize the "***CATS Movement Philosophy.***"

COMMUNICATION, ADAPTATION, TRANSPORTATION, STABILISATION

C.A.T.S. MOVEMENT PHILOSOPHY

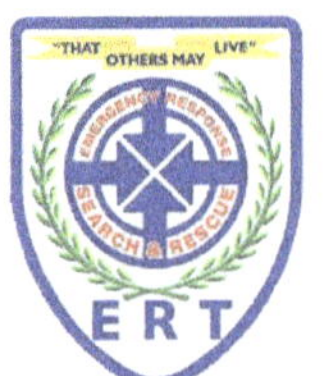

- Static Locations
- Buildings and Structures
- Heavier Vehicles Post / Static
- Larger and Heavier Equipment
- Designated purpose items
- Specific Training for Conditions

- Mobile Teams & Persons
- On Foot or small structures
- Smaller Vehicles or Mobile
- Smaller, Lighter Kit
- Multi Purpose items
- Improvisation based on situation

In disasters and emergencies; The closer you get to the Incident, the rescue, the patient,
The more mobile you will be. The less kit and equipment you will carry,
The more flexible you may need to be.

Incident Movement and Kit Philosophy
© 2002 / R. 2017 Gary Foo

SEARCH Mnemonics

1 This image we did to illustrate the process of the acronym, L.A.S.T. with the clear demonstration of at least 2 in the SAR team.

Here are many mnemonics from SAR Basics.

L.A.S.T.

The acronym LAST is used as a mnemonic for SAR (Search and Rescue) Operations.

- Locate
- Access
- Stabilise
    - Emotional
    - Medical
    - Physical
- Transport

Foo's 5 types of Missing Person

1. Lost
2. Missing
3. Abducted
4. Seized
5. Absent

Establish Search Area

- Theoretical
- Statistical
- Subjective
- Deductive Reasoning

Lost Person Behaviour

- Profiling
- Investigating
- Planning
- Operations

Passive Search

- Track Traps
- Confinement
- Magnets
  (N.A.P. Natural, Artificial, Personal.)
- Attraction etc.

Active Search

These are the start of active searches and not the only types or terms.

- **Type I**
  Hasty / Initial Response
- **Type II**
  Efficient, Sweep Searches or Open Grid
- **Type III**
  Thorough or Closed Grid Search
- *Specialist*
  i.e., Trackers, Sign Cutters, Forensics

Type II Search Team ("Efficient")

The objective is to cover the mapped sectors or geographical areas rapidly but efficiently. A Type II Search is done by using efficient techniques by trained resources. The general search area is usually systematically broken down into search sectors which are geographically distinct. For example:

- **ROUTES,** like roads and paths
- **BOUNDARIES,** like hedges and fences
- **AREAS,** like fields or open areas
- **PLACES,** like buildings, homes or shops

Route Searches

- Roadways and highways /motorways
- Paths / Tracks
- Ditches
- Hedges
- Boundary
- Watercourses (look over to opposite side.)
- Down side roads 50m+
- 2 searches: same side or opposite side?

Corridor Searches

This is a search which penetrates into a boundary or area parallel to the route and path along that 'line.' It is basically a wide "R&P" (Route and Path) search.

Area Search

Developed in Canada & US and adapted for UK (mainly by Mountain Rescue).

- Define boundary / sectorise
- Hasty Teams
- Type II searches – Critical Separation
- Classic Line
- Creeping Line
- Expanding spiral
- Searching Slopes / Hills
- Always stop periodically and also look all around. Remember the "Searchers Cube."

Boundary Searches

- Hedges, Fences, Perimeters, etc.
- Hedges give good shelter
- Consideration for Alzheimer's
- Search 15 meters in (used to be 5m)
- Watercourses: again look to opposite side of bank
- Body may be carried
- 2 searches go up or 'leapfrog'

Search of a place

- Buildings
- Shops
- Malls
- Houses (Permission. Favourite places?)
- Inhabited (Caution)
- Derelict (careful)
- Outbuildings
- Car Parks
- Industrial Premises

Other Searches

Also Consider possible circumstances (like a child abduction) or possible mechanisms i.e., Sri Lanka Body Search after tsunami.

- Rely on intelligence gathering
- Logical Reasoning
- Forensics
- Evidence Trail
- Science: i.e., Physics in motion (Water)

Purposeful Wandering

The term for searching a large area in a general line where the team of 3 to 6 searchers covers an area delineated by landmarks, often not a route (road, path or trail) as specified during the briefing.

The team may make several parallel *sweeps* through the area. The team member at one end of the line guides the team from the known landmarks, while the member on the other end marks the extent of the *sweep* with flagging tape.

RESCUE STANDARDS: NFPA 1670, 1006 & 1983

There are very many NFPA standards you may know. Very Commonly it's Firefighter I & II from NFPA 1001. And there is NFPA 472 for Haz-Mat, NFPA 1041 for Fire Service Instructor and NFPA 1021 for Fire Officer. Many more too … but the the following are commonly known standards for NFPA Technical Rescue. If you teach or provide Tech Rescue you should know these standards. You can freely see them online at www.NFPA.org and download for a fee.

- NFPA 1670: Standard on Operations & Training for Tech. Search & Rescue Incidents, 2017 Edition
- NFPA 1983: Standard on Life Safety Rope and Equipment for Emergency Services, 2017 Edition
- NFPA 1006: Standard for Technical Rescue Professional Qualifications, 2017 Edition

NFPA 1006 Chapters 2017 – Part 1

NFPA 1006 2017 Edition – Chapter Summary
Chapter 4 to Chapter 12 and Chapter 13 to Chapter 22

NFPA 1006 Chapters 2017 – Part 2

NFPA 1006 2017 Edition – Chapter Summary

DEFRA FLOOD RESCUE MODULES (UK)

Training standards for Water and Flood Rescue

The following modules define the appropriate training for water related activities.

Module 1: Water & Flood Awareness	General water safety awareness training
Module 2: Water & Flood First Responder	To work safely near and in water using land based and wading techniques
Module 3: Water & Flood Rescue Technician	Specialist rescue operation
Module 4: Water & Flood Rescue Boat Operator	Rescue boat operations
Team Commander	Water team related incident command
Module 5: Water & Flood Incident Management	Water-related operational and tactical incident command
Module 6: Flood Rescue Tactical Adviser	Provide advice to tactical and strategic commanders and credentialing
Module 7: Flood Rescue Strategic Adviser	Provide advice to the National Flood Response Centre and Strategic Coordinating Groups

Note of DEFRA Requirements in ERT SAR

In general, ERT SAR Members should be Module 3 and Module 4 to satisfy our requirements as a Type B and C team under DEFRA.

Those who are MOD 1 or 2 should be actively doing this in pursuit of getting to Module 3 and / 4.

We also would like to have some higher such as Module 5 (Water & Flood Incident Management).

The next page is from the DEFRA Flood Rescue Concept of Operations. (DEFRA FRCO) AKA DEFRA Flood "ConOps."

TEAM TYPE	CAPABILITY
A Amalgamation	• Amalgamated teams • These will be known as A – B for powerboats and A – C for mixed teams • Teams of this nature are not pre-declared but are established during the incident with members and equipment from assets from the National Asset Register • An example would be embedding a health care professional[10], police officer, or RSPCA member in a B or C team
B Water & Flood Rescue Boat Team	• Technical water rescue • Search operations within the water environment • Powerboat rescue operations • In-water operations • Flood response
C Water & Flood Rescue Technician Team	• Technical water rescue • Search operations within the water environment • In-water operations • Non-powered boat operations • Flood response
D Water & Flood Rescue First Responder Team	• Support operations • Limited in-water operations • Bank-based safety and search • Flood response

Although the National Asset Register only has team types B and C, the criteria for team type A and team type D are also outlined in Table 1, and the minimum requirements for a team type D are set out in the team typing matrix in Annex J.

A team type A is an amalgamation of two or more declared assets to meet a risk or community need. An amalgamated team could be formed with responders from different organisations to address a specific need, as required. These teams would be identified as 'A-B' for an amalgamated team which meets team type B specification or 'A-C' for an amalgamated team which meets the team type C specification.

LRFs routinely hold a list of local flood rescue assets. it is recommended that local assets also meet the team typing standards for B, C and D teams to better enable local and national assets working alongside each other during an incident. As part of their response to a flood incident. LRFs should utilise local assets identified within their MAFP before they access assets on the National Asset Register. Further information on requesting assets and how assets are mobilised is outlined in Annex B.

---

[10] For the purposes of this document. "health care professionals" generally refers to paramedics and doctors with pre-hospital emergency care qualifications sand/or /experience.

Rope Log

Keep a rope usage log (or PPE / harness or even personal training log) by using this CMC table

ROPE LOG

Date in Service: _____________________   ROPE NUMBER _______________

Length: _____________ (ft)   Diameter: _______ (in)   Rope Color: _________________   Bag Color: ___________

Manufacturer: ___________________   Model: __________________   Tensile Strength: _______________

	Date	Incident/Location [a]	How Used [b]	Possible Damage [c]	Inspection Results	Sign In
1						
2						
3						
4						
5						
6						
7						
8						
9						
10						
11						
12						
13						
14						
15						
16						
17						
18						
19						
20						

a. Include activities such as operations, trainings, inspections, and washing.
b. Detail use of the rope such as for rappel, rappel rescue, main line, and system belay.
c. Did something happen that may have damaged the rope such as rock fall, impact load, severe abrasion, sar other abuse?

© 2014 CMC Rescue, Inc.

DISASTER

Learn and know the disaster management cycle. ERT SAR is capable in all 4 quadrants and provides enhanced capacity building, and community resilience, but trains for Disaster / SAR in the "Response."

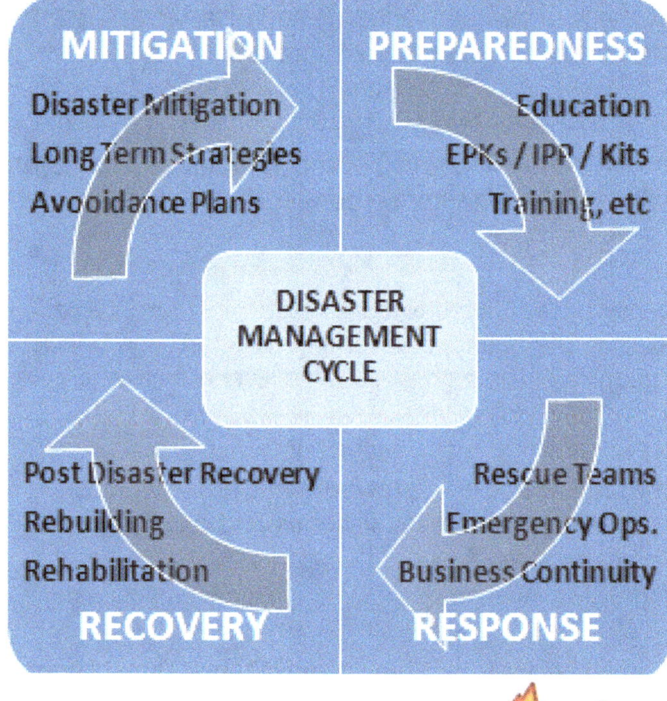

Mitigation:
- Measures that prevent or reduce the impact of disasters.

Preparedness:
- Planning, training, and educational activities for things that cannot be mitigated.

Response:
- The immediate aftermath of a disaster, when business is not as usual.

Recovery:
- The long-term aftermath of a disaster, when restoration efforts are in addition to regular services.

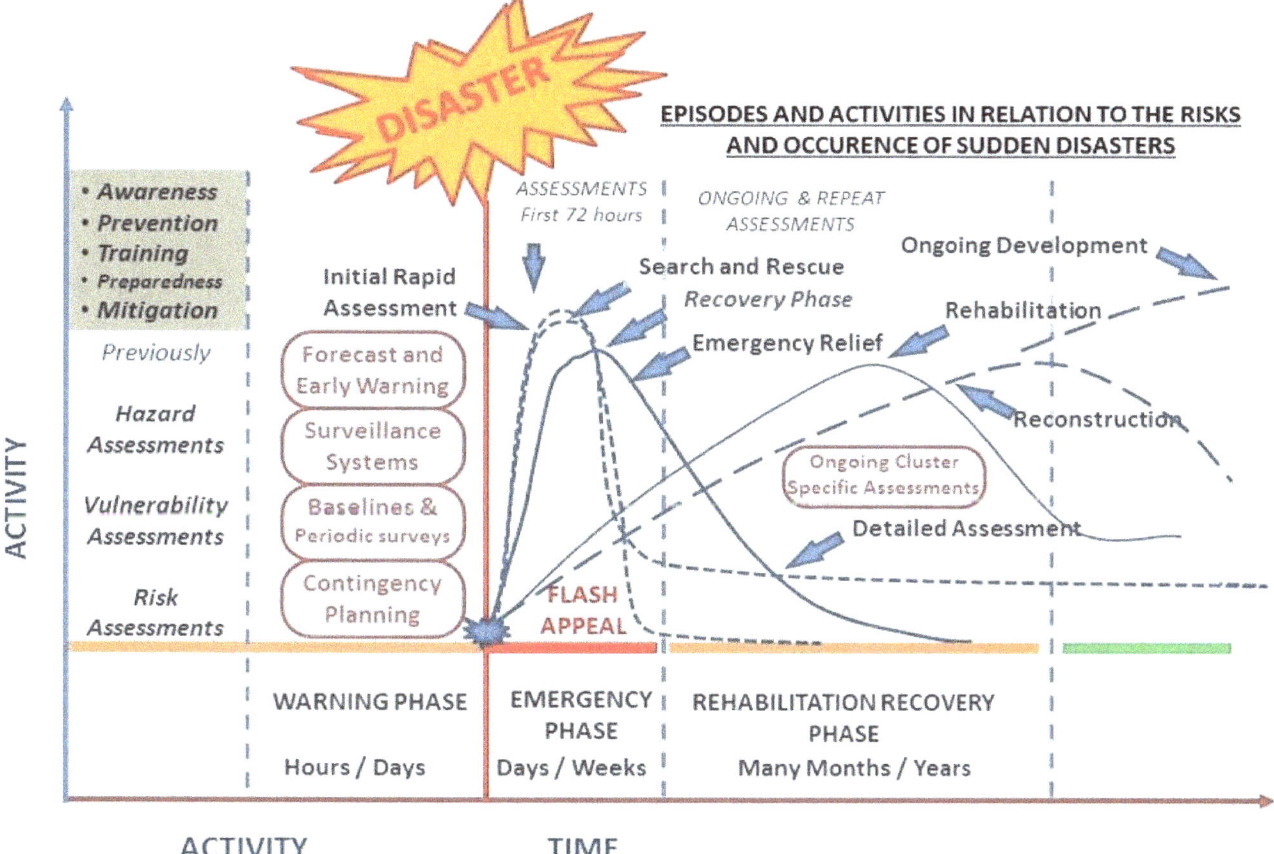

3 A modified self-explanatory graph we developed and built on from existing ones out there.

Disaster Standards and Relevant International Groups

Here are a few groups and organisations (some made from acronyms),

UNITED NATIONS

Commonly referenced for many humanitarian practices or rescue standards and disaster assessments especially in regard to OCHA (Office for the Coordination of Humanitarian Affairs)

INSARAG

Standards for the "International Search and Rescue Advisory Group" and commonly referenced for international USAR / Structural Collapse standards in global disaster response.

WHO

The World Health Organization is a specialized agency of the United Nations responsible for international public health. The WHO Constitution, which establishes the agency's governing structure and principles, states its main objective as "the attainment by all peoples of the highest possible level of health."

DEFRA

Stands for The Dept for Environment, Food and Rural Affairs is the government dept responsible for environmental protection, food production and standards, agriculture, fisheries and rural communities in the UK but in this context is reference for Flood Response / Rescue standards.

FEMA

The Federal Emergency Management Agency is an agency of the United States Department of Homeland Security ref. Disaster standards.

NFPA

National Fire Protection Association standards from the U.S. regarding Fire & Rescue relevant methodologies and best practice especially NFPA 1670, 1006 & 1983 in context of rescue.

Disaster & Emergency Response Vaccinations

First Responders, especially international disaster SAR / First Responders are often asked which inoculations they should have. Apart from personal hygiene, *and depending where you are going*, it is expected you would have or consider certain vaccinations.

In ERTSAR the following are the first recommended, especially before any international deployments:

- Yellow Fever, for which vaccination is a requirement for entry into certain countries.
- Tetanus, in combination with diphtheria.
- Poliomyelitis.
- Hepatitis A and Hepatitis B.
- Typhoid.
- Cholera (taken before departure).
- Meningococcal meningitis.

There are other vaccinations according to the disease's endemic in the area of the world being visited, that should be considered: For example: ***Anti-Malaria, Japanese encephalitis, rabies*** etc.

Remember to take all possible precautions against becoming unnecessarily exposed to these threats or risks and get information on the local area. One of the most basic preventative actions is to avoid contaminated food and water and try to avoid getting bitten by mosquitoes etc.

KIT LISTS

ERT SAR provided the following reminders of useful kit lists and what they carry. Members are smart, professional and prepared. This is an important part about the capacity of ERT SAR as an organization.

It is common to see well organized and labelled personal kit in member's bags as well as organized and labelled kit and equipment in the lock up and holds.

TEAM PROPERTY LOCK UPS

In general team kit and equipment is stored in locations which are listed by two letters and a number.

- **e.g. AB 1 or Alpha Bravo 1**

Items will be photos graphed in situ and balled in bulk and put on the team inventory app.

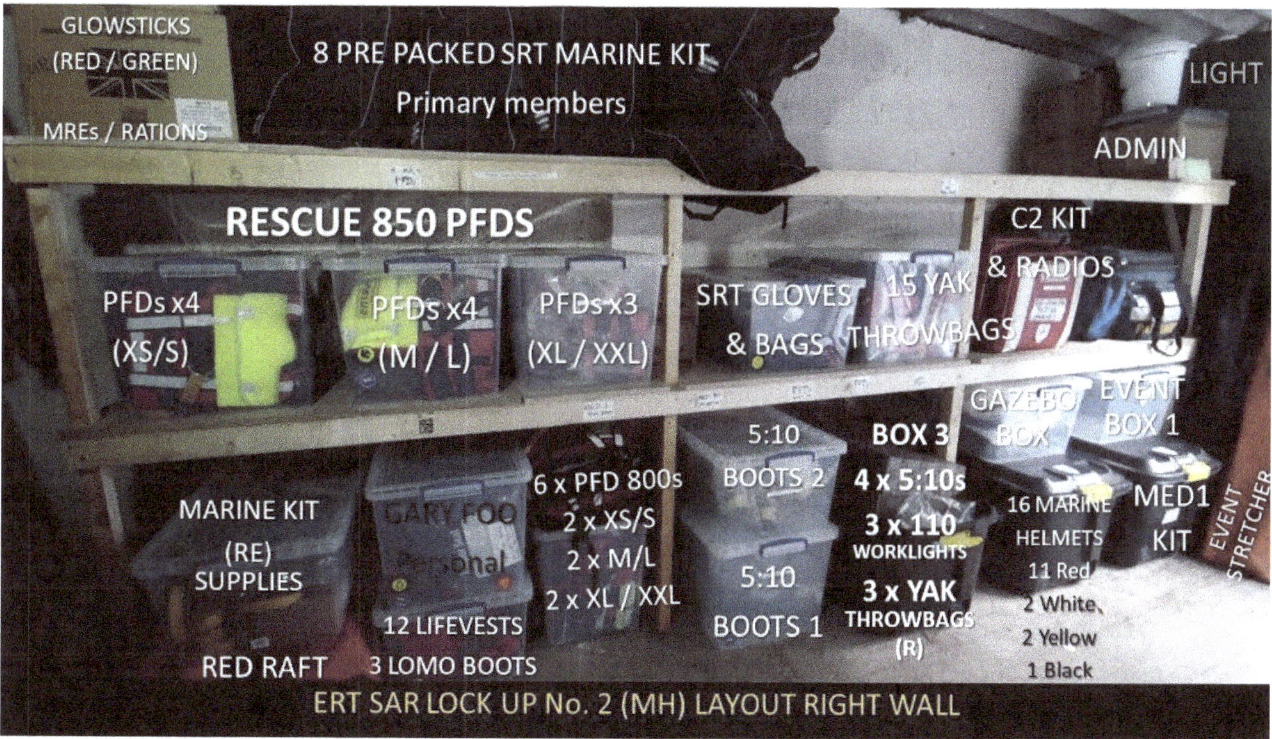

NB: Inventory is usually performed annually every February as well as any major adds or minuses.

Personal Kit

Remember the closer you get to the "action" the less you will be able to carry unless you have a very heavy supportive kit, equipment and logistics section. Members personal kit is carried and organised in 5 main areas, which should be labelled.

- Tab Bags
- Utility Bags
- Grab Bags
- Duty Belts
- On Person

G1098

What is the G1098?

This is our term but based on the British Military term.

The G1098 is a 'tip of the hat' term to the old British MOD (Ministry of Defense) form for QMS (Quarter Master Stores) supplies form.

In our context is a modern version of "minimum kit and resupply items" as well as survival kit.

This is usually in a small (see through) pouch and contains items that you will need to have on any SAR or Emergency Response mission.

4 A G1098 pack. It is in a transparent "Medical" pouch. You can also buy see through 'Make Up Bags' from the shops. This pouch is about 7.5 inches X 5 inches X 3 inches and packed full! As per SOP, it is labelled with the owners name and what it is.

This is your essential SAR list of kit in a small or a few small packs like transparent bags. Some of it will actually be on your person / in your pockets but you would possess this. The mini-multipurpose kit that was carried everywhere (all members have something like this.) All SAR teams have bits and bobs and whistles and compasses and extra pens etc.

This is *in addition to* what's carried. In other words, the whistle, compass, 2 black pens and notebook, etc. in the G1098 is a backup for redundancy and *in addition to* what's *already* carried.

It won't necessarily have all these items but commonly have most if not all these.

- It is part SAR essentials
- It is part ERT SAR min. kit
- It is part "preppers" survival bits
- It is part resupply or redundancy back up

DID YOU KNOW? … "B SQUAD & SAR ENGINEERS"

Did you know that SAR Engineers have technically got a specialist section called "specialist SAR Engineers which includes Specialists in SAR, like SAR Dog Handlers, Vehicle and Engine Mechanics, and those who use vehicles as a part of SAR Response!

An example is the "Mobility Troop" within SAR Engineers who are Specialists in different forms of transport such as SXS (Side by Side), 4X4 (Four by Four / Off Road / 4-Wheel Drive), Motorcycle uses, towing a trailer, etc. They would be able to do most! (Originally these were SAR TECHS only but now also Specialist SAR Engineers!)

G 1098 List

You can use this list as a template or an example.

- ☐ Notebook
- ☐ 2 Black Pens
- ☐ 1 permanent Marker
- ☐ Digital Memory Cards
- ☐ Torch / Flashlight
- ☐ 2 Glow sticks
- ☐ Small Knife
- ☐ Mini-Fire kit
- ☐ Windproof lighter
- ☐ Flagging Tape
- ☐ Duct tape (on card)
- ☐ Superglue
- ☐ Cable Ties
- ☐ Bungie Cord
- ☐ Paracord (25-50 ft)
- ☐ Nitrile Barrier Gloves
- ☐ Ear Plugs
- ☐ Bin bags/Rubbish bag
- ☐ Zip lock sandwich bag
- ☐ Eating Utensil / Spork
- ☐ Batteries (extra spares)
- ☐ Multitool
- ☐ Another whistle
- ☐ Another small Compass
- ☐ Hand Sanitizer
- ☐ Pocket Tissues
- ☐ Toothbrush & paste
- ☐ Dental Pick
- ☐ Mints / sweets
- ☐ Mini Deodorant
- ☐ Nail clipper
- ☐ Mini-Sewing Kit
- ☐ Surgical Blade
- ☐ Wet/dry sandpaper
- ☐ Vaseline / Lip Balm
- ☐ Small Analgesic pills
- ☐ Mini Tape Measure
- ☐ Mini Key 'Biner
- ☐ Small Groundsheet
- ☐ Small Crocodile Clips
- ☐ Combination Padlock

Mini-First Aid Kit

A minimum (pocket) first aid kit list. This is IN ADDITION to a proper First Aid / Med Kit.

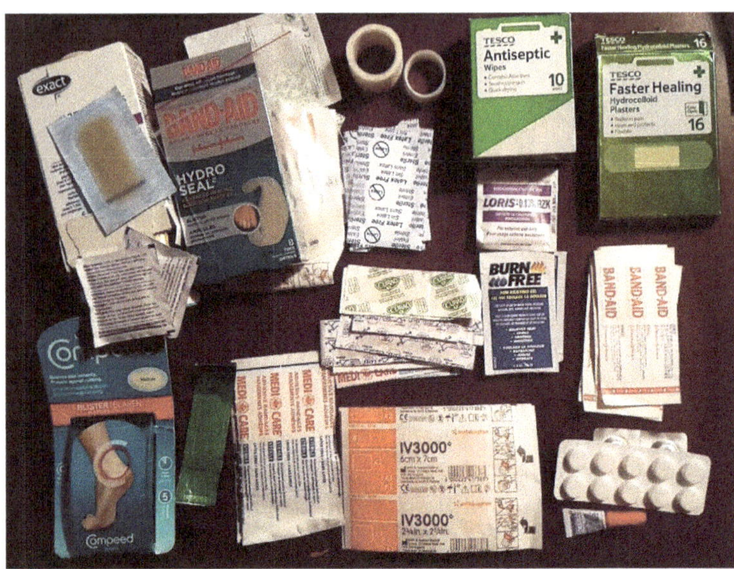

- Antiseptic Wipes
- Band-Aids / Plasters Small
- Band-Aids / Plasters Medium
- Band-Aids / Plasters Larger
- Meapore Dressing
- Non-Adherent Pad
- Small Hydrocolloid Dressing
- Burn Gel sachet
- Blister Pads
- Micropore Tape (small roll)*
- Duck tape (small card)*
- IV 300 Dressing *
- Surgical Blade *
- Skin Glue *
- Analgesic (Pain Killer) Pills
- Tooth pick / Nail clipper

*Requires training. Not always carried.

IFAK Medical Kit

For those of you who carry them, depending on your level of training and ability, would consider carrying an IFAK or Individual First Aid Kit. A standard IFAK Medical kit list. This is IN ADDITION to a proper First Aid / Medical Kit.

IFAK KIT Min. Contents include:

- 1 x TQ (CAT Tourniquet)
- 2 x 4" or 6" ETD (Israeli or Olaes)
- 2 x NAR Z-Fold Gauze / Celox
- 1 x Hyfin Vented chest seal, Twin pack
- 1 x Nasopharyngeal Airway, 28f
- Paramedic Sheers / EMT Scissors
- Glowstick/s
- ARS Needle / Needle D (re: Needle Thoracentesis for Tension pneumothorax (TPX))
- Gloves, Tape & Black Sharpie Marker
- Firm Eye Shield
- PRF (Patient Report Form) or CCC (Casualty Care Card AKA TC3 CCC)

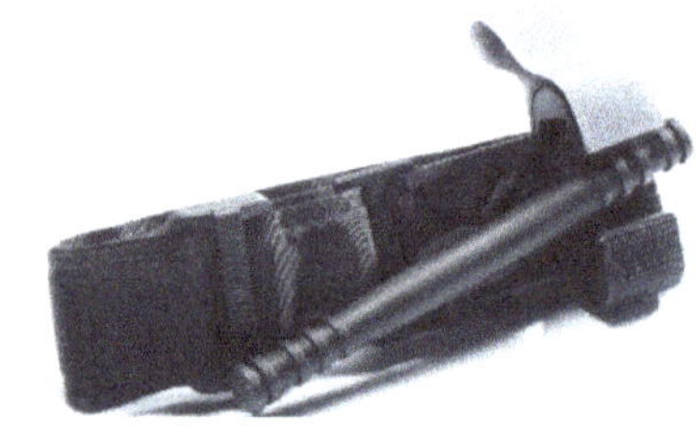

CAT - Combat Application Tourniquet (Gen 7)

Level 1 PPE

Standard Kit (Low level impromptu / Brief exposure / lower risk. Refer to Infection Prevention Control & PPE Document)

- 2-3 Face Masks N95+
- 2-3 sets Nitrile gloves
- 2-3 Pairs of ear plugs
- Riggers gloves (lite)
- Eye protection (clear)
- Hand sanitizer
- 2 Glow Sticks
- Head torch
- Spare batteries
- Hi-Vis Vest *(Optional)*
- Black Knee Pads
- Helmet (Gallet/Manta)
- Hi-Vis Vest *(Optional)*

MARINE UNIT PERSONAL KIT & EQUIPMENT

In general, all marine unit members wear their uniform as standard uniform on land with their ranks, badges and markings to represent that they are on the Marine Unit.

The **YELLOW ERTSAR Label** is often associated with the Marine Unit. (The Black version is used by the whole organization and all ERT SAR members.)

PERSONAL KIT LIST (BOLD indicates members might thet their own kit here.**)**

1. Water Rescue Helmet
2. PFD: Rescue 800 / 850 (Some members get their own.)
3. **Rescue Knife (blunt & tethered)**
4. **Pealess Whistle (Fox 40)**
5. ***Waterproof Watch & Compass**
6. ***Waterproof Light & Headtorch**
7. Waterproof Radio (issued)   →
8. Cow Tail (Tether)
9. Water Rescue Boots
10. ***Water Rescue Gloves (Neoprene)**
11. Dry suit (Red with Logos)
12. "Woolly Bear" Fleecy
13. ***Glowsticks / lights (red, white, green)**
14. **Throwbag – YAK 20m**
15. ***Food / Snacks & water**
16. ***Polarised Sunglasses** *(Reduces Glare)*
17. ***Waterproof notebook & 2 Pens**
18. ***Navy Blue Cargo Shorts (fast dry)**
19. ***Black wicking fast drying T-shirt**
20. *Full change of uniform & towel
21. ***Small Marine First Aid kit**
22. ***All in a DRYBAG (Red or Black)**
23. **Optional: Neoprene skull cap*
24. *Optional: Marine Distress Flares etc*
25. *Optional: Wetsuit*
26. *Optional: Goggles / mask, snorkel & Swim fins*
    1. ***A: Personal Hygiene kit:***
    2. ***inc. Toiletries,***
    3. ***SPF 50 waterproof suncream,***
    4. ***Personal hygiene inc. hand sanitizer, * mouthwash etc***

ALL The ERT SAR Marine Kit in a picture

The list on the previous page can be pictorially represented below.

GENERAL MARINE PERSONAL KIT

1. Water Rescue Helmet
2. PFD: Rescue 800 / 850
3. Rescue Knife (blunt & tethered)
4. Pealess Whistle (Fox 40) & swim goggles
5. *Waterproof Watch & Compass
6. *Waterproof Light/s & Headtorch
7. Waterproof Radio (issued)
8. Cow Tail (Tether)
9. Water Rescue Boots
10. *Water Rescue Gloves and a carabiner
11. Dry suit (Red with Logos)
12. "Woolly Bear" Fleecy
13. *Glowsticks / lights (red, white, green)
14. Throwbag – YAK 20m
15. *Food / Snacks & 1- 2 ltr Water & Purifier?
16. *Polarised Sunglasses
17. *Waterproof notebook & 2 Pens
18. *Navy Blue Cargo Shorts (fast dry)
19. *Black wicking fast drying T-shirt
20. *Full change of uniform & towel
21. *Small Marine First Aid kit
22. *All in a DRYBAG (Red or Black)
23. *Optional: Neoprene skull cap
24. Optional: Marine Distress Flares etc
25. Optional: Wetsuit
26. Optional: Goggles / mask , snorkel & Swim fins

Just the personally ERT SAR Marine Kit highlighted in a picture

The list on the previous page can be pictorially represented below.

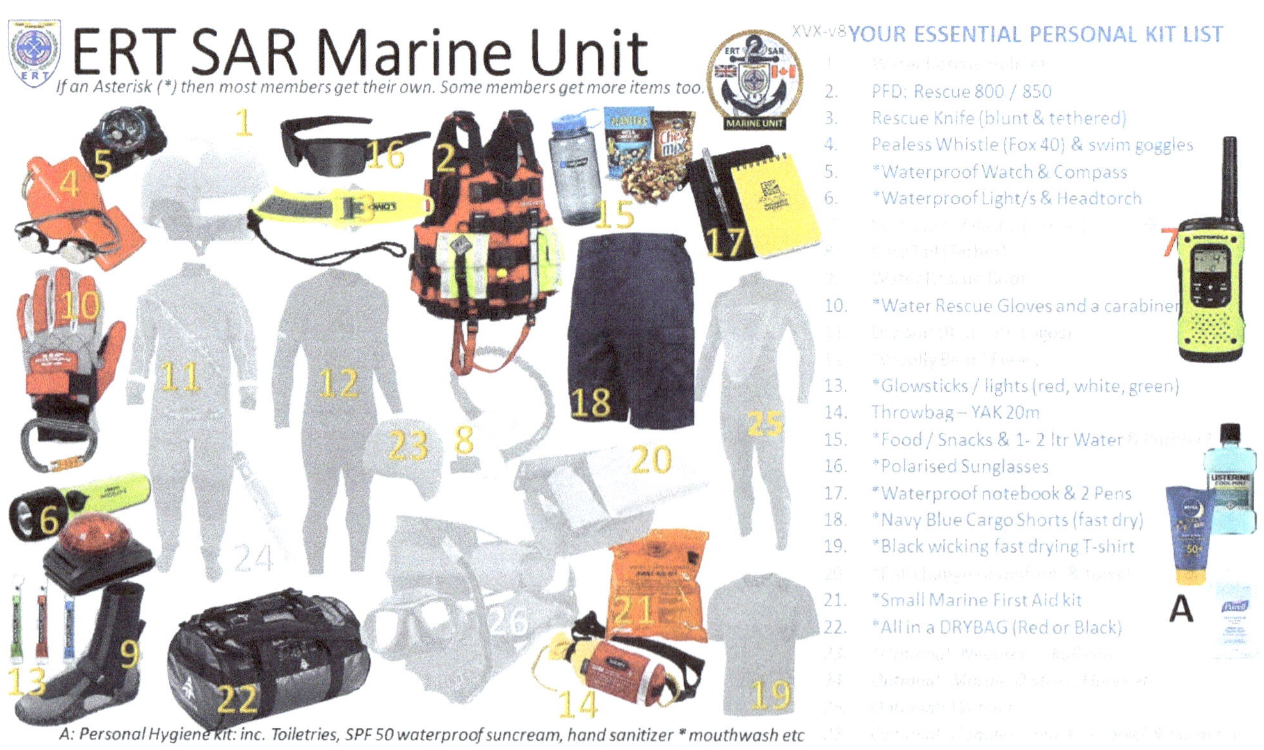

YOUR ESSENTIAL PERSONAL KIT LIST

2. PFD: Rescue 800 / 850
3. Rescue Knife (blunt & tethered)
4. Pealess Whistle (Fox 40) & swim goggles
5. *Waterproof Watch & Compass
6. *Waterproof Light/s & Headtorch
10. *Water Rescue Gloves and a carabiner
13. *Glowsticks / lights (red, white, green)
14. Throwbag – YAK 20m
15. *Food / Snacks & 1- 2 ltr Water
16. *Polarised Sunglasses
17. *Waterproof notebook & 2 Pens
18. *Navy Blue Cargo Shorts (fast dry)
19. *Black wicking fast drying T-shirt
21. *Small Marine First Aid kit
22. *All in a DRYBAG (Red or Black)

Distress Communication

ERTSAR Marine Unit members need to know and recognize **the COLREGs - Preventing Collisions at Sea Convention (on the International Regulations for Preventing Collisions at Sea, 1972**.) In particular the **Rule 37 (Distress signals)**

This is when a vessel is in distress and requires assistance she shall use or exhibit the signals described in Annex IV to these Regulations, in the graphic below.

J: How to get fully badged in the Marine Unit

Being a member of the Marine Unit is prestigious and not automatic. Many members apply and get to train with or as a part of the Marine Unit. The following gives an outline of what to do to become a *Full Member of the Marine Unit* and also how to get *"Fully Badged" as a member of the unit.*

				Signed / initialed, Name & Date
			Operational Member (Signed off OTC2 sheets)	
			Member asserts that they can swim & emails interest	
DATE	DATE	DATE	Passed Uniform Inspection (3 times)	
DATE	DATE	DATE	Passed Kit Inspection (3 times)	
			Passed Enhanced Fitness Test (& in-date at the time)	
		MUP 1	Classroom Theory Session (1/2 Day)	
			**Now you can start coming out to Marine Unit (Amphibious) sessions to become a Full Member**	
		MUP 2	Practical Boat Launch (1 Day)	
		MUP 3	Practical Rescuer in Pool Session (1 Day)	
			Marine Unit Specific Team Training Session 1	
			Marine Unit Specific Team Training Session 2	
			Marine Unit Specific Team Training Session 3	
			Marine Unit Specific Team Training Session 4	
			Marine Unit Specific Team Training Session 5	
			Marine Unit Dirty / Wet Session 6 (done in any order)	
		RadOp	VHF Radio Licence (SRC / ROC-M)	
			Pass Written Test based on Marine & ERTSAR SOPs	
			Pass Practical Evaluation	
			Now you are a *Full Member of the Marine Unit*	
		Medic	e.g. Marine Medical (RYA First Aid)	
		F.A.S.T.	SRT (Swiftwater Rescue Technician)	
		Cox	RYA PB II / PCOC (tested)Powerboat Cox	
			Now you are a *"Fully Badged" member of the unit.*	

SOME ADDITIONAL AND RELEVANT MARINE UNIT QUALIFICATIONS CAN BE INITIALLED BELOW if appropriate.

MEDA3	SVOP	ICE RSQ	MOD 4	RYAPBA	DIVER	TOW	OR 4X4	OBS FF	Helo HI
Marine Medical Emergency Duties 3	Small Vessel Operator Proficiency	NFPA Ice Rescue Technician	Flood and Swiftwater Boat Operator	Royal Yachting Assoc Advanced Powerboat	Diving Qualified Rarely needed. Not recreational	Can comfortably Tow boat on a vehicle trailer	Off Road all and 4-wheel Drive trained capable	Firefighting capable on boat ship / board	Heaving In lines & Helicopter Operations

International Kit List

SAMPLE D SQUAD / INTERNATIONAL KIT CHECKLIST

This is a reminder checklist and not necessarily ALL mandatory or all inclusive.
DEPENDING ON THE MISSION PROFILE

Items in *Italics*, are optional

BAGGAGE / BAGS for personal kit
Everything inside *(label)* compartmentalized

- ☐ 1 Black ERTSAR Grab Bag (i.e. Condor 125)
- ☐ 1 Black / Coloured large "Tab Bag" rucksack
- ☐ 1 Follow on/Utility Bag
  (Could be Red Marine drybag)

- ☐ Duty belt w/ at least 3 pouches
- ☐ (A black bag for duty belt for when not worn)

Note you should pack in plastic zip-lock bags
Or in Vacuum pack compression bag/s
Or zippered "clothing cubes" or combination of (and ideally with labels)

If Capacity Building type mission it is usual to have a Civilian Suitcase / Wheeled trolley as pictures above otherwise it's grab bag, tab bag, and utility bag. CBM

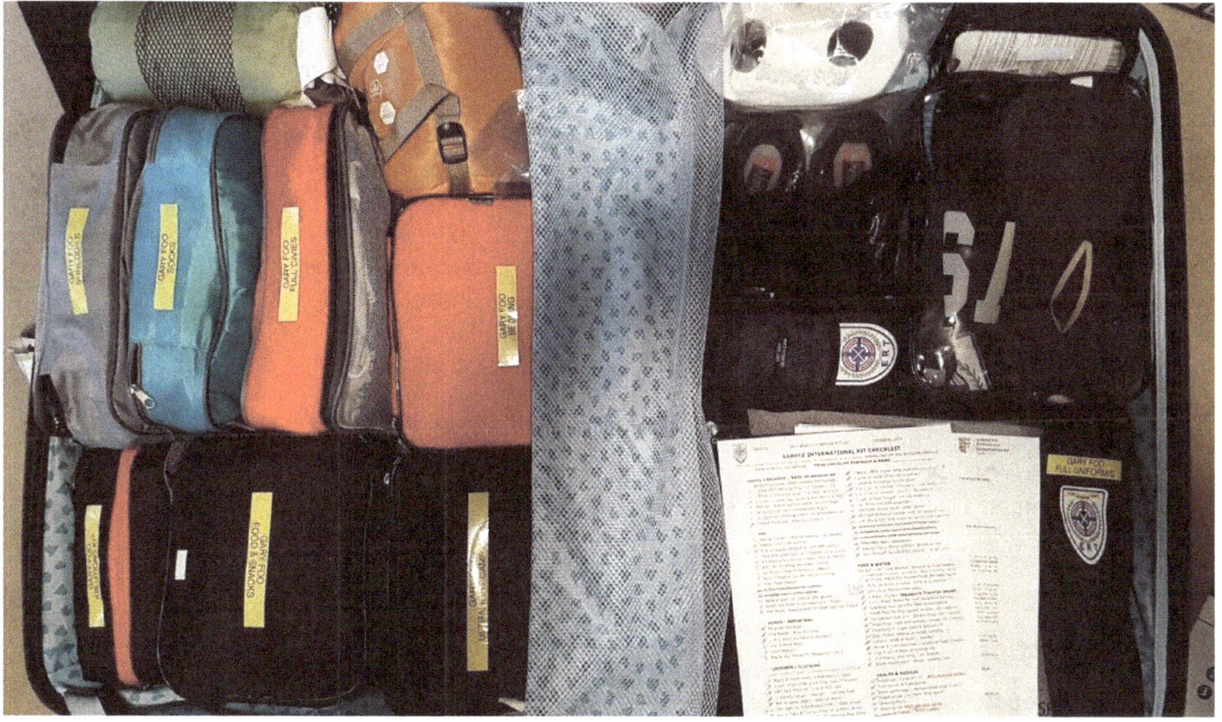

5 In this sample photo you can see that packing clubs and clothing bags are labelled and all contained providing additional organisation and protection.

International Packing List Continued

This is a good foundation checklist we use for general ERTSAR deployments. This may be adapted and modified by the seniors in charge depending on the mission but this is a good foundation list.

PPE

- ☐ Helmet (Gallet / Marine Helmet – as issued)
- ☐ Helmet torch / Headtorch
- ☼ Sunglasses (i.e., Wiley-X or w/ PPE ability)
- ☐ Clear Eye protection (or Goggles) 1 or 2 prs
- ☐ 4-5 Mouth/face shield masks (N95 or better)
- ☐ APR (Air Purifying Respirator) Mask
- ☐ Ear Plugs / (Ear Defenders) (Many)
- ☐ Work / Riggers Gloves (debris moving)
- ☐ Knee Pads (Black)
  - ❋ Thin thermal (under) gloves
  - ❋ Outer warm winter gloves
- ☐ Several pairs of medical PPE gloves
- ☐ Small handheld bright flashlight / Torch
- ☐ Hi-Viz Reflective Bands
- ☐ Hi-Viz Reflective Vest / Tabbard
- ☐ PPE Boots: Waterproof? Or Steel toe? Etc

Helmets:

As a rule the following guidelines apply

TYPE / STYLE

Gallet   USAR (First Choice or Red Manta Pros)

First choice: Rope Rescue Tech / USAR

Manta   Water Rescue
       Ice Rescue
       Rope Rescue
       Seadoo / PWC

COLOUR

White   Incident Commander / Leader / Motorcycle
Blue   Gallet Helmets: Technicians / USAR
Red   Water Helmets: Technicians (Or Rope)
Yellow   Water Helmet: Operators / Responders
Black   Instructors (sometimes)

Admin / Reporting

- ☐ Personal Notepad (waterproof pages?)
- ☐ 1 or 2 Black permanent markers
- ☐ 2 or 3 Black Pens
- ☐ Crib Sheet / Aide Memoire
- ☐ Plastic Zip Wallet / bag (for Passports / Cash)
- ☐ (Passport usually worn at all times cargo pocket)

Admin kit (depending on mission)

- ☐ Local Map/s? local language & briefings etc
- ☐ ERT SAR Kit & Sticker Labels
- ☐ ERT SAR Waterproof Humanitarian Aid Labels
- ☐ ERT SAR Colour Banner/s
- ☐ ERT SAR Car Magnets
- ☐ ERT SAR Window Decals
- ☐ ERT SAR Business Cards
- ☐ ERT SAR SWAG? (pins, patches, coins, etc.)
- ☐ USAR Aide Memoire (Know Markings)
- ☐ USAR TECH SEARCH KIT (Search Cam/DelSAR)

Misc. & Operational Tools

BE CAREFUL. Not on airline carry on
- ☐ Multi-Tool knife (Pliers, Screwdrivers, Wire-cutter etc.) Handtools, folding sierra saw, etc.
- ☐ Paramedic Shears (Medical Scissors)
- ☐ Cutting Instrument / Rescue Knife
- ☐ Padlock /cable / cable - Ties to secure kit?... ?
- ☐ Orange spray paint / fat marker

Team Kit

(depending on mission)
Kit usually in cases and labelled
- ☐ Team Solar Lights
- ☐ Honey Bucket / Honey Seat (2)
- ☐ Wag Bags for Toilet (Honey Seat)
- ☐ Toilet Tent
- ☐ Sanitary Cleaning
- ☐ Shovel / Spade
- ☐ Team Tents (Half number for rated capacity)
- ☐ Gazebo & Banner (1 or 2)
- ☐ Ground sheets / Tarps
- ☐ Cots / Lilos?
- ☐ 2-4 ltrs of water per person / day
- ☐ Satellite Phone
- ☐ Thermal Imaging Camera
- ☐ Night Vision Goggles
- ☐ Personal Locator Beacons
- ☐ DEPLOYMENT MARINE / RESCUE KIT
- ☐ DEPLOYMENT USAR KIT & TOOLS
- ☐ Chainsaws
- ☐ Generator/s
- ☐ DEPLOYMENT MEDICAL KIT
- ☐ Medical Needles, cannulae, airways, O2?
- ☐ Emergency Team Medic Drugs

Hygiene, Health & Medical

- ☐ Deodorant (stick/roll on - **NOT aerosol spray**)
- ☐ Toothbrush & Toothpaste
- ☐ Body wash soap / Multipurpose soap (tube?)
- ☐ Bodypuff / cloth (to increase wash lather
- ☐ Towel or pat dry micro fibre towel
- ☐ Shaving Razor
- ☐ Shaving Gel NOT aerosol spray
- ☐ Electric shaver
- ☐ Unbreakable Mirror
- ☐ Comb / Brush
- ☐ Lip balm / Skin cream / moisturizer
- ☐ Toilet Roll (for you for duration of mission) CBM
- ☐ Personal body wipes / tissue
- ☐ Body deodorizing shower wipes /Baby Wipes
- ☐ Sanitary Towels / Pads (Ladies)
- ☐ Personal Medical Kit & Medicines *i.e. Malaria*
- ☐ Spare Glasses (if you wear glasses / contacts)
- ☐ *Dental Kit:* Toothpicks / Dental flosser
- ☐ Mini-Sewing Kit (black & blue cotton)
- ☐ Few small rubbish bags in kit & hazmat bags
- ☐ Few large Garbage / Bin / Rubbish Bags
- ☐ Mosquito Nets
- ☐ Sunscreen SPF +50
- ☐ After Sun
- ☐ Insect / Bug Repellent
- ☐ After bite / itch relief

Valuables & Money

- ☐ Passport (with 6 months or more on it) &
- ☐ 2 copies of it **
- ☐ Vaccination Log / WHO Yellow booklet
- ☐ 4 to 6 Small passport sized photos
- ☐ Country Visa (or similar **IF** required)
- ☐ Some US / local Currency &
- ☐ & credit card / Debit Card with credit card logo
- ☐ Money Belt (worn under uniform)
- ☐ A (Robust Waterproof) Watch
- ☐ **Save documents & Credit cards to cloud

Remember to back up a lot of these documents in the cloud and ensure you have copies if needed.

Marine Unit Members note that valuable documents carried should be in waterproof pouches or double sandwich bags to reduce damage by water / sweat etc

Food & Water

DO NOT USE "ADD WATER" Rations as main supply!

CBM Food supplies usually reduced on Capacity Building mission

- ☐ 8-10 day MREs Pre-Packed Food (No water req'd)
- ☐ 2 to 4 litres of water / day (500 ml v 2L bottles)
- ☐ ORS (Oral Rehydration salts)
- ☐ 1 Water Purifier (Aquapure Traveller issued)
- ☐ 1 (+) Water Bottle for belt (Nalgene / Stainless)
- ☐ Snacking food bars for daily consumption
- ☐ Fresh fruit for first couple of days (NB Customs)
- ☐ Foil packed fruit (i.e., Child's food) *(NB Customs)*
- ☐ Dried Fruit, nuts and snacks / treats *(NB Customs)*
- ☐ Chocolate in sugar shell & biscuits (?)
- ☐ Cup (Plastic folding or metal camping ~)
- ☐ Cutlery: Knife & Forks / Sporks
- ☐ Stove & Fuel (Optional. Careful w/ fuel) Customs
- ☐ Cup & set of Pans or boiling cup
- ☐ If bringing cans bring Can Opener
- ☐ Water Purification: filters / tablets / etc.

Survival / Sleep Items

☼ ❆ Sleeping bag rated for the weather
- ☐ Underpad / inflatable Mattress **(depends)** CBM
- ☐ Pillow/s / Inflatable **(depends)** CBM
- ☐ Pea-less Emergency Whistle (min x2)
- ☐ Compass (also consider GPS)
- ☐ 7 to 10 Glow Sticks (Various colours)
- ☐ Lighters/Waterproof Matches/Flint Stick
- ☐ Candles / Tea lights
- ☐ DUCT Tape (Packed down)
- ☐ Paracord / Cordage (25 ft or more. i.e., X2)
- ☐ Liner / Emergency Thermal Blanket (?)
- ☐ Fish hooks & Line
- ☐ Sewing kit
- ☐ Survival knife (with full tang)
- ☐ Multipurpose Glue/s
- ☐ Fabric Glue / Super Glue *(Gel)*
- ☐ Wire saw?
- ☐ Extra 'layer' sheet / wool blanket / silk inner

LEADERSHIP & MANAGEMENT

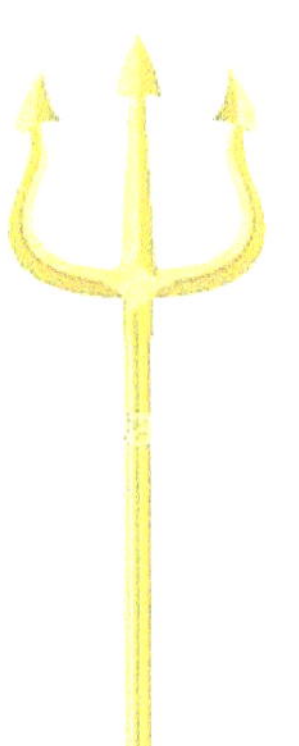

There Three Essential Operational Leadership Mandates to Remember:

1. Safety & Welfare of the whole team and controllable factors within it
2. Mission Objective or Achievement in conjunction with the first mandate,
3. Standards of Operation whether, SOPs, or International standards, KPIs, Correction & Commendation, etc.

Leadership and Management: The (Marine Unit) Trident 3

The Trident is very symbolic in mythology. It is known as the weapon of Poseidon, or Neptune, the God of the Sea in classical mythology.

In ERT SAR's Marine Unit the "Trident" spear is sometimes used to represent certain aspects of ethos or operations, like Amphibious operations in the **Air, Sea (water) and Land.**

It is also sometimes used or referred to as the 3 essential aspects for ERTSAR's SAFE AND SUCCESSFUL MARINE OPERATIONS.

SAR Chief, Gary Foo quoted this upon starting ERT SAR saying that it was essential to meet certain operational objectives whilst keeping people safe and operating with established standards, SOPs / SOGs and operating parameters. So, in summary that represents:

1 Safety of the team (and others)
2 Mission Achievement / Successful completion of Objective
3 Ensure Standards

Many others use the symbol from "Aquaman" to the United States Naval Special Warfare Command, and the Special Warfare insignia. It is particularly worn by members of the US Navy SEALs, and a trident represents the three aspects (Sea, Air, and Land) of SEAL special operations.

The Trident is on our Marine Unit Challenge Coin and Award has two crossed Tridents on the front of one side.

6 ERT SAR Marine Unit Meritorious Award Challenge Coin

So, in some ways the crossed two represent the

OPERATIONAL TEAM LEADERSHIP 3 above
AND
The fact that we are an Amphibious team of specialists. We deliberately did not call ourselves a "Water Rescue Team" or anything like that. That would be good for some but untrue for ERT SAR. Our "Amphibious Operations and Capacity" means that being a "Marine Unit" is more reflective of our team and *raison d'etre.*

Doing the Trident 3 may be synonymous with checking the 3 aspects of Leadership and Management of the team listed above. Safety & Welfare, Objective and Standards.

Briefing and debriefing

Briefings must provide the essential items of information, including what is to be done, who is to do it, how it will be done, where and when it will be done.

Bear in mind this briefing may have the luxury of a weather proof structure and well-prepared briefing board, but it can equally be delivered outdoors near the incident site.

Planned: GSMEAC

- **G** Ground
- **S** Situation
- **M** Mission
- **E** Execution
- **A** Admin / Logistics
- **C** Command / Communications

Emergency: STICC

- **S** Here's what we face
- **T** Here's what I think we should do
- **I** Here's Why
- **C** Here's what we should watch
- **C** Now, talk to me...

Giving a SMEAC Briefing

A briefing must be given concisely, clearly, confidently and in the correct sequence. It must provide the essential items of information including:
- what is to be done
- who is to do it
- how/where/when it will be done.

Post-incident assessment

A key element of organizational risk management is the timely and effective assessment of incidents and accidents. These should be investigated to determine causality. ERTSAR employs structured methods to identify the causes of failures and implements lessons and changes that may prevent reoccurrences, such as:
- near misses
- accident reports
- lessons learned.

Debriefing and Correction

Non one should be afraid of owning up for their mistakes and in fact it is encouraged as a learning and sharing tool. Admitting areas to work on means that you have learnt what you did wrong and shares with others which means it may reduce the chance of it happening again.

Incident debriefing

The power of any debrief should never be, but often is, underestimated.

Debriefing helps us to:
- ensure the welfare of our team at the end of any service, training or exercise
- ensure the equipment is accounted for, operationally ready or defect reported
- ensure any lessons learnt from the event are captured
- develop the team involved to perform even better next time.

Even after a training session it is good to have a training debrief. The communication helps members gel and gain team spirit whilst supporting each other's learning.

G SMEAC BRIEFING FORMAT

(G) SMEAC is an acronym which breaks into the following headings:

G Ground / Operating Environment
(This is sometimes included in the "S")

S Situation
A brief description of what is happening/happened:
- Ground
- Hazards
- Weather
- Other agencies
- Event

M Mission
What is the actual objective of the task?
The mission brief should be short, using simple language that everyone can understand:
- Our mission is …
- In order to …

E Execution
- Tasking: Assign jobs/roles and team allocation.
- Equipment: The equipment required and allocated.
- Limitations: The factors that may restrict options.

Emergency plan:
The plan in the event of an emergency or non-standard operation: • General outline • Grouping/tasks

A Administration
What administrative arrangements and logistic support have been put in place:
- Dress/PPE
- Equipment
- Food/Water
- Medical
- Transport
- Casualty routine/Evacuation

C Command and communications
Issue and clarify call signs and radio frequencies and identify the chain of command and communication:
- Type
- Call signs
- Lost comms
- Ops normal
- Confirmation of understanding
- Questions?

We have some great long form examples of this method we teach on Leadership Courses!

(G) SMEAC Briefing Template

SITUATION:
- Ground:
- Hazards:
- Weather:
- Other agencies:
- Event:

S

MISSION:
- Our mission is:
- In order to:

M

EXECUTION:
- General outline:
- Grouping / Tasks:
- Emergency Plan:

E

ADMINISTRATION:
- Dress:
- Equipment:
- Food / Water:
- Medical:
- Transport:
- Casualty routine
  / Evacuation:

A

**COMMAND,
COMMUNICATION
& CONFIRMATION:**
- Type:
- Call signs:
- Lost comms:
- Frequency/Talkgroup:
- Ops normal:
- Confirmation of
  understanding:
- Questions?

C

7 We have been using this format, although usually the GSMEAC since about 2007 / 2008 however we would like to thank the RNLI for this version template.

UNIFORM: Reminder of Uniform Dress

How members look, their dress, deportment and visual representation says a lot about them. It creates an impression. It shows 'professionalism' and discipline and PPE etc. It creates a sense of team spirit and pride. Here are a few reminders of uniform standards. Refer to the SOP document (such as the SOP1 uniform etc. document) for a fuller resource.

- Upon joining members get a round neck shirt *(Guardian Shirt)*
- You can wear a log sleeved wicking shirt underneath is you like.
- You should wear the rest of your uniform smartly like usual with good boots, belt, etc.
- Usually you can wear your Polo shirt when you are C squad and / or Marine Unit / D Squad
- Polo shirts are worn with your BLACK wicking undershirt (not bear skin)
- Polo shirts are worn with Country flag on right shoulder / sleeve
- Country flag is positioned about 5 fingers from seam
- Rescue Tech Badges are worn by Rescue Techs, with your **Medical Badge** underneath
- Polo shirts usually have just the first button done up
- Polo shirts are ALWAYS tucked in
- Polo shirt is ironed with the crease facing forward (not folding badges in half.)

How to wear the Polo Shirt

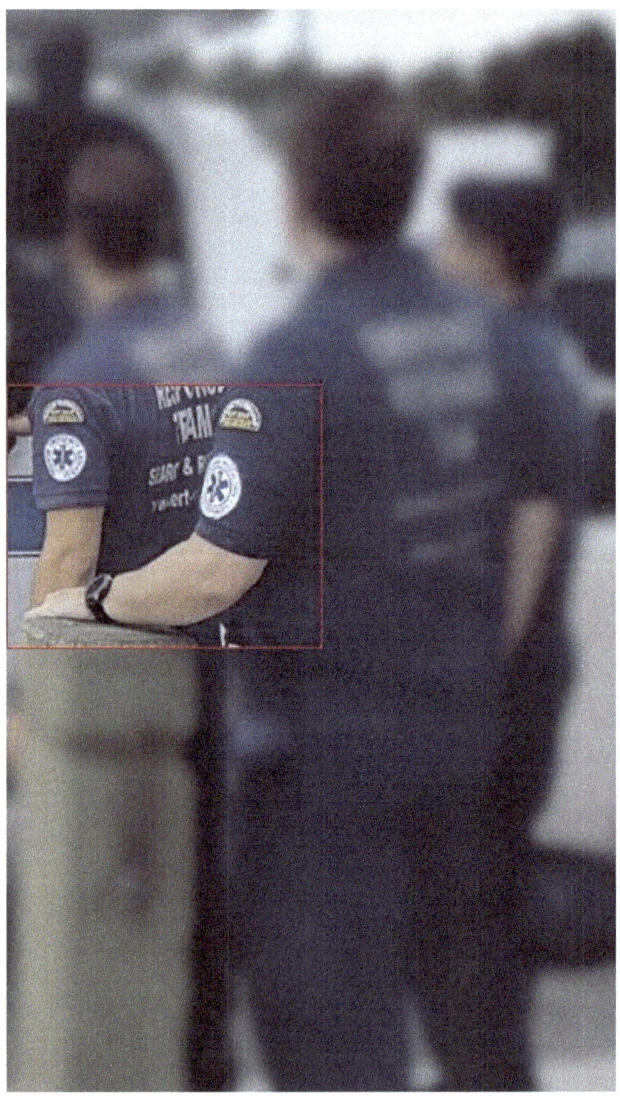

ERTSAR LOGOS & ICONS

April 2004, Revised regularly since in several forms.
THIS VERSION: 19 – 14 August 2020
Corrected from 18 for typos and Marine Unit Member Badge

When used by the Marine Unit this badge is usually "Yellow" and black ad contrasting in Colour.

E-Mail: HQ@ert-sar.com

The ***Emergency Response Team Search and Rescue*** is a humanitarian disaster and emergency response Search and Rescue team, Non-Profit Organisation and Registered Charity.

Our motto is "That Others May Live"

This document may not be reproduced without the prior consent of ERTSAR except for the personal use of the member and in no way should there be a commercial / financial gain by anyone doing so. ERTSAR takes no responsibility for any outcomes as a result of this manual.

Photos & Graphics: ERT SAR / Gary Foo

MARINE UNIT BADGE SUMMARY
Fouled Anchor: (As opposed to an Anchor)
The specialist abilities of the member to resolve marine situations and extensive training and ability.

Crossed Tridents: Trident 1 is the Amphibious Water, Land and Air & Trident 2 is the Safety, Operational capacity & Standards, The are crossed' and signify respect of the waters, back up & strength.

Colour: The subdued grey colour is the low key and manner of work doen to a high level for others and not selfishly or for recognition. All are volunteers.

Border: The Rope Wrap border signifies, skill, marine and unusual types of situations resolves with skill and knowledge and tenacity and resolve. Collectively: Specialist Amphibious Ability and Dedication with strong Team Work & Discipline.

THIS IS THE ERT SAR LOGO

GUARDIAN MEMBER LOGO

MARINE UNIT LOGO

MARINE UNIT
QUALIFICATION "BADGE"

Summary Log of Training Certifications

Please use this if you wish as a hard copy record of your training

Award Date	Expiry Date?	SUBJECT / DISCIPLINE & LEVEL	Source
		NFP! 1006 CH. 5: Rope Rescue - Technician Level	
		Swiftwater Rescue Technician – [Mod 3	Tech Level]	

ROPE RESCUE AIDE MEMOIRE GUIDANCE

TACTICAL CONSIDERATIONS
PHASE I Arrive On-Scene. Take Command. Size-Up.

A. First Arrival. The first arriving ERT SAR C / D SQUAD Technical Rescue "Captain" or "Senior Most" Member would assume and be known as **"Command"** after arriving on the scene.
- **Do a quick size up especially environmental safety and sitrep.**
- **Assign Safety and Cordon Off Working Area if known**
- **Create a priorities and tactical plan. Adjusts as necessary given conditions.**
- **As always plan for victim / patient PPE as a part of the kit needed at point of care.**

B. ANY & ALL Tactical Front-Line Operators and Rescuers should be wearing their last resort belt (Ideally CMC rated belt) with Rescue webbing and carabiners.
- **RESCUE TECHS** (with shoulder badge) wear 20 – 22 feet of black 1" rated webbing
- **SAR TECHS** (who wear the SAR Tech Badge) carry above but in Red.
  - *Minimum two to four T-rated carabiners*
  - *Ideally harness (Class 3) and multitool (on lanyard) with descender and prussic cords*

A. **IMPORTANT:**

SAFETY TIE OFF FIRST!

ERTSAR members will consider and if necessary, establish a travel restraint or simple anchor system for themselves before going to the edge of any opening, height, ledge, drop or similar hazardous fall area.

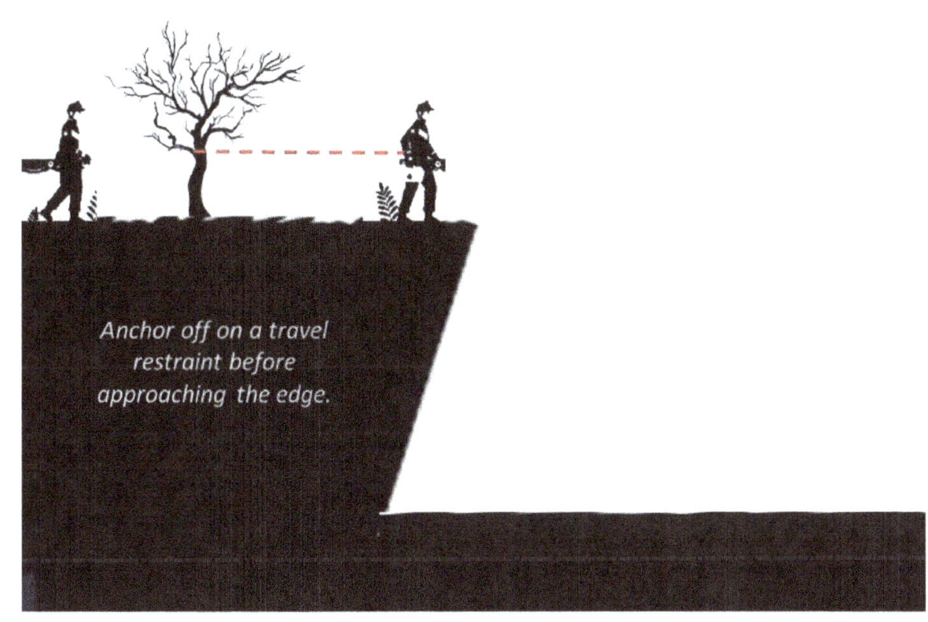

- SAR TECHS carry RED WEB lanyards and webbing and could use that.
- RESCUE TECHS can use black. ALL Operational Members can use any rated rope or travel restraint system to anchor to their Harness or even last report belt if needed.

B. BEFORE you approach any edge or possible fall hazard, ensure you are 'connected' to some form of fall arrest system with a solid anchor. In other words, if about to enter a hot zone with a possible height, drop, loop out, opening (like a conspace drain) or steep slope etc. the immediate thoughts should be to find a secure anchor point and then connect a travel restraint / fall arrest (even if improvised with the webbing) to ensure that the risk of falling is mitigated.

Organising and Staging your Rope Kit

How to Organise your Rope Kit

We have organised our kit and equipment many ways over the years. Remember to …

- Name and label, it
- Have a Kit List
- Pack it logically
- Put where you can get easily
- Put where you can get it quickly
- Put it where you can pack up easily
- Put in a container which protects it.

We are currently using a heavy duty shoe organiser with labels which hangs on the side of the van or on a tree (after a cord has been erected.)

The Use of Staging Tarps

Usually you will need a "Staging Tarp." A Staging Tarp is not only a way to place items on a surface which might protect it, such as on the wet grassy or muddy ground.

The Staging Tarp may also be great at laying everything out and having 'labels' of what should go where. Remember to put out a 'weather cover'.

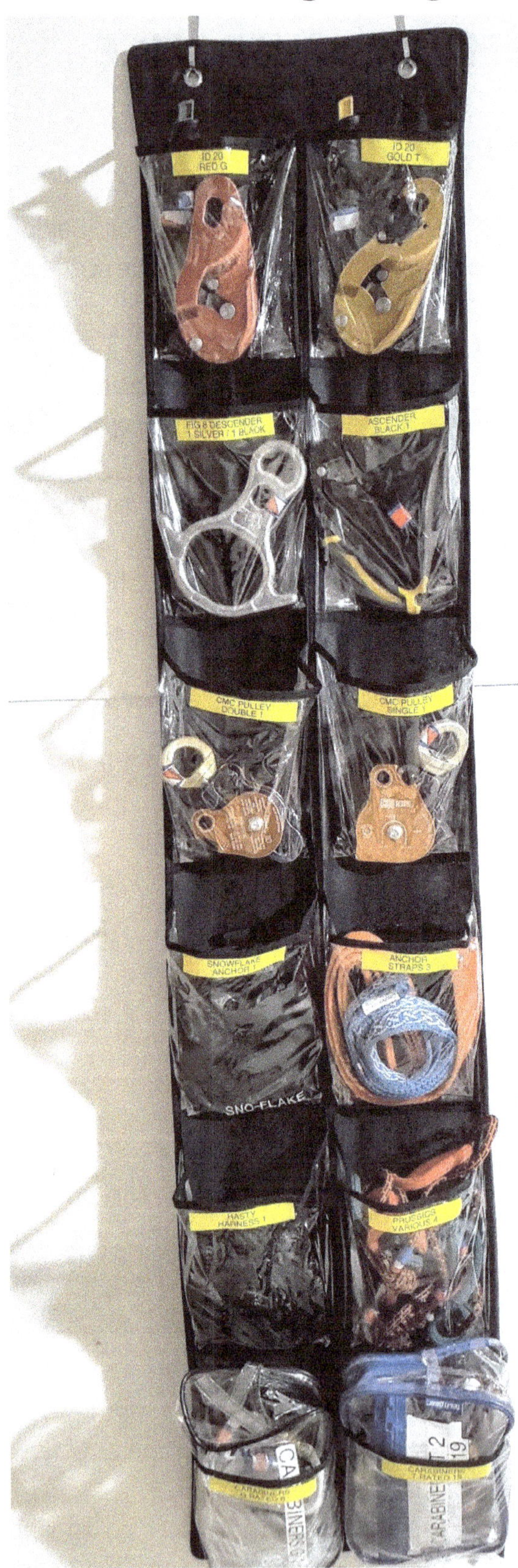

8 We are currently packing some kit in easy to see and access heavy duty durable 'shoe organizers' and you can see it and it is labelled so you can also see when it is "out" and needs to be brought back.

9 Weather Cover over a Staging Area

NAME OF CANDIDATE

SAR OPERATOR (GUARDIAN) CHALLENGE / OTC2

Upon successful completion of Part 1s to 4, the Candidate will be deemed to have met the minimum standard for Operational Capacity in National Disaster and Search and Rescue Incidents, at the SAR Engineer / Responder Level and eligible to wear the ERTSAR Polo Shirt.

THIS IS THE ANSWER KEY VERSION. IT IS NOT PREFERRED FOR TESTING BUT IS USED DO NOT SHOW ANSWERS WHEN QUESTIONING THE CANDIDATE AND THEIR RESPONSES TO BE EASY.

ERT SAR CANDIDATE ASSESSMENT & OTC2 2020

This new standard updates and replaces all previous versions of the OTC (Operational Training Course) and where discrepancy exists in the SOP Manual or other documents, then this version will be considered correct. If run intensively and consecutively would take at least 3 to 5 days. Challenge equivalency permitted in parts.

To be initialed by Approved Senior Leader / Captain / Commander

The purpose of this document is to check that the Candidate is knowledgeable, skilled and equipped for ERT SAR Operations. Upon successful completion the Candidate is awarded the NEW 2019 **ERT SAR Disaster Response and Search and Rescue L2 OTC Certificate**

Reaching the Standard will be recognized by an ERT SAR Certificate and a special custom Digital Badge
Completed by combining a variety of input and throughput methods the Candidate will be taught and also prove knowledge, skills and readiness through Face to face testing, evaluation, questions and answers, displayed, skills demonstration, proof of knowledge, completion of written tests, reading texts, Distance eLearning (DeL), watching videos, reading other materials, manuals, books, etc.
Ultimately the Candidate will be awarded a Certificate, a Digital Badge and also a Challenge Coin

PART I: Inspections, standards & checks.
Prerequisites to be completed before attempting the practical test day

PART II: Practical Test Day.
Demonstration of required knowledge and skills on the OTC

PART III: Foundation Knowledge.
To be completed _at any time_ before, during or after the OTC Test day (and some on equivalency)

PART IV: Uniform & Kit Check.
Required minimum uniform standard and minimum kit list before being operational.

Do not formally assess until ready. Candidates may be pre-evaluated at any time convenient to invigilator/s. All skills are to be performed safely and confidently in from of an approved ERT SAR Standards invigilator.

	Signed & Dated
This document only requires ONE signature / Initial: **Successfully Completed.** Validated by ERT SAR Invigilator	

OFFICE USE ONLY Certificates Awarded	YES / NO	Date	Sent ___ / ___ / ___	By

Thee should be scanned and preserved softcopy as well as fire hard copy and details logged on ERTSAR Intranet

PART 1: INSPECTIONS, STANDARDS & CHECKS

NOTES	USUAL PREREQUISITES AND INITIAL QUALIFICATIONS TO ENTRY	INITIAL	DATE

Prior to attending the OTC or formal training the following is checked.

☐ **Provided all proof of ID (Passport / Driving License)**
Check this once you have seen it. Copy sent to DOCS@ert-sar.com

☐ **Provide supporting documents (i.e., Relevant Certificates)**
Check this once you have seen it. Copy sent to DOCS@ert-sar.com

☐ **Produce proof of recognized First Aid and CPR training or equal to ~**
Check IN DATE when seen. Copy sent to DOCS@ert-sar.com

☐ **Downloaded Member Log Matrix or has FOG Aide Memoire Book**
Check this once you have seen in candidates possession (name on it)

☐ **Responsiveness: Actively responds to TeamApp, e-mail, text etc. last 3**
Check this once on the TeamApp at last few notices and attendance

☐ **Doesn't sign up last minute or fail to show or cancel last minute. Last 3**
Check this with ERT SAR Records. Cancelling last minute especially
more than once does not show a dependable availability.

☐ **Possesses an ERT SAR Uniform Coat with Country Flag on right shoulder**
Check this once you have seen it. (Flag should also be on Polo Shirt.)

☐ **Candidate can recognize a definition of SAR and the 2 main types**
Basically, we are looking for Search and Rescue in a Disaster
environment such as Collapsed Structures of Buildings (USAR) and also
SAR for Lost and Missing Persons. They should have also read and be
familiar with FOOs 5 TYPES OF LOST AND MISSING PERSONS.

☐ **Candidate knows Intl. symbol for Civil Defense and functions & roles**
The international distinctive sign of civil defense, defined
by the rules of international humanitarian law and
to be used as a protective sign.

Historically included several functions such as
rescue, medical, planning, coordination,
"Warden" etc. in a Civil Defence / Civil
Protection mode not unlike the "Emergency
Services" of today and some countries this remains.

PART 1: INSPECTIONS, STANDARDS & CHECKS

NOTES	BASICS BEFORE DUTY: COMMUNICATIONS AND ADMIN	INITIAL	DATE

☐ **Candidate produces a notebook with starting duty completed**

Notebook 'should' be waterproof or lined and page numbered.

Usually full date, weather, road, environment, type of duty & names of

pertinent people (i.e., Leader / Instructor / team partner etc.)

This is observed and signed off by an authorized senior member

☐ **Candidate understands why numbered pages are required.**

"Should" have numbered pages explained that it may be used in

evidence & is less likely to add / remove such evidence after the fact.

☐ **Candidate understands the concept of *contemporaneous notes***

"Notes made at the time or as soon as practicably possibly after"

☐ **Candidate can complete an Operational notebook entry for duty**

This is Checked and observed and signed off by an authorized senior

member for 2 to 3 recent "Attendance" times on a Notebook Check.

☐ **Demonstration of the ability to perform a radio check and use a radio**

Letter and number (if more than one) assigned.

(Call sign of SAR Chief, ST3 & Command / Control maybe 'names')

<u>Tester:</u> Golf Foxtrot to Control, Radio Check?

<u>Control:</u> You are 10-2 (Loud & clear.) "How you receiving me, over?"

<u>Tester:</u> You are 10-2 also. Out.

Short, simple. clear. If it is not good then it is "10-1" and fix the issue.

☐ **Knows all the International Phonetic Alphabet (A to Z)**

Tester should randomly select 3 to 5 letters & response should be fast

☐ **Knows the ABC of Radio Use & example of a "10-30"**

☐ A = Accurate, B = Brief & C = Clear

☐ 10 = 30 is misuse of radio and would include unprofessional casual

'banter' and chirping along with bad language, profanity, private

details on air, victim / casualty details on air, inappropriate or secure

information being passed on, etc.

<u>*NOTE: There is a way to pass on secure information using ten codes or*</u>

<u>*secure means or a method taught to SAR CAPTAINS & ST3s*</u>

☐ **Knows [1] single and [2] repeated whistle blow, meaning in ERT SAR.**

Single Whistle is usually "Attention!" or "Look at me" (Person blowing)

Repeated whistle blows = "Emergency!" sometimes "Evacuate!"

PART 1: INSPECTIONS, STANDARDS & CHECKS

NOTES	DRESS, DEPORTMENT & UNIFORM PARADE & UNIFORM STANDARDS	INITIAL	DATE

Has read and attests to the importance of standards in a professional group

☐ **Read the S15 (No drinking, no drugs, no discrimination etc)**

Member shows they have it.

This is observed and signed off by an authorized senior member

☐ **Read Candidate's code of conduct (Responsiveness, Proaction etc)**

Gives a few examples of S15

This is observed and signed off by an authorized senior member

☐ **In uniform *Candidate can* Stand at Ease**

This is observed and signed off by an authorized senior member

☐ **In uniform *Candidate can* Stand to Attention and**

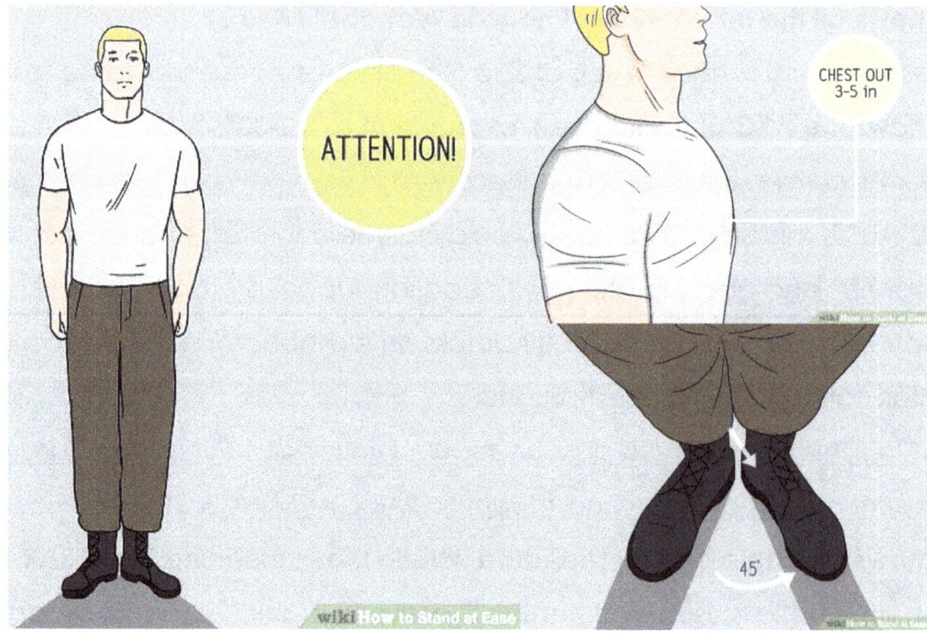

This is observed and signed off by an authorized senior member

NOTES

☐ **Salute (ERTSAR is Naval style usually with Cover (Hat/Helmet) on)****

1. The "style" is palm down like the naval officer is doing below.

2. She is also wearing a hat. We usually salute with "Headcover" on.

   (However we DO salute without Cover and indoors if warranted.)

3. We usually stand to "Attention" when Saluting.

This is observed and signed off by an authorized senior member

☐ **Knows when to use 'hand on heart' instead of Salute**

If in Civilian Dress, No "Cover" (Hat) and some circumstances like that

This is questioned & signed off by an authorized senior member

** NOTE:
Salutes are not usually given with no cover (no hat or helmet on) by may do.

PART 1: INSPECTIONS, STANDARDS & CHECKS

DATE	CARRIED KIT: POSSESSES, THE FOLLOWING ITEMS <u>ON PERSON</u> *Candidate should have a kit list and be working to achieve it. (Check mark)*	INITIAL	DATE

Usually on person

- ☐ Watch (Waterproof) *
- ☐ Notebook *
- ☐ 2 Black Pens *
- ☐ Permanent Marker *
- ☐ Whistle *
- ☐ Compass *
- ☐ Phone / smartphone *
- ☐ Mini-First Aid *
- ☐ Personal meds / analgesics *
- ☐ Cutting Instrument (Knife)
- ☐ Paracord / Cordage (Min 10-12 ft) *
- ☐ Torch / Flashlight *
- ☐ Small Phone Charger & Cable
- ☐ Money / Bank Card *
- ☐ Reflective Hi-Viz (PT) Yellow Bands (Coat)
- ☐ ID Card (worn right waist level) &
- ☐ PAS (Personal Accountability)
- ☐ ERTSAR Dog tags (only if issued).

If there are 4 or 5 items missing, they can pass with a note that the list is short

Usually to hand eg Belt kit *also cf. grab bag*

- ☐ 1 Day Food (Nonperishable e.g. MRE)
- ☐ Snacks and refreshments
- ☐ Drinking Water (Minimum 2–6 Ltr / day)
- ☐ Sunglasses / Safety glasses
- ☐ Mini-Fire kit (Fire starters)
- ☐ A lighter (ideally Windproof)
- ☐ Flagging Tape
- ☐ Duct tape
- ☐ Superglue
- ☐ Few Cable Ties
- ☐ Bin bags / Rubbish bag
- ☐ Eating Utensil
- ☐ Multi-tool
- ☐ Head-torch
- ☐ Glowsticks (min. Red / White / Green)
- ☐ Few Pairs of Nitrile Gloves *
- ☐ Paramedic / EMS Sheers / Scissors
- ☐ Ear Plugs (Noise Pollution)

INITIAL

If there are 4 or 5 items missing, they can pass with a note that the list is short

*Items with an asterisk are mandatory and must be possessed by the OTC in order to pass this inspection. The other items not mentioned like Firestarter / Lighter etc. & may be elsewhere such as belt kit or grab bag. **A FULL Candidate Kit List is listed in the SOP Manual and the FOG Aide Memoire.**

- ☐ *This is observed and signed off by an authorized senior member*

PART 1: INSPECTIONS, STANDARDS & CHECKS

NOTES	CONCEPTS OF SEARCH AND RESCUE (SAR) & SURVIVAL CLOTHING	INITIAL	DATE

☐ **Will be able to explain what is "PPE" with some examples**

PPE is Personal Protective Equipment like gloves, masks, earplugs etc. and designed to provide a level of protection against certain hazards

☐ **Can explain why, in general, cotton is an inappropriate fabric for SAR**

The saying is "Cotton Kills" & in most cases it is inappropriate because it absorbs a lot of water & does not wick. *(Some cotton is better now.)*

☐ **Will bring and possess "layers" in uniform operations**

Wicking (Merino wool or synthetic sports undershirt) with uniform shirt followed by warming and ERTSAR coat. _Outer layer always ERTSAR._

☐ **Will be able to recite the 3 W's of clothing + 1 (Weather check)**

1: Wicking 2: Warming 3: Weatherproof (like Wind and Rain proof.)

☐ **Can explain pros & cons of down filled versus synthetic (polyester)**

Down Coat / Sleeping Bag: Lightweight, warming. Not so when wet. Synthetic Coat / Sleeping bag: Heavier, warming, still useful when wet.

☐ **Can state benefit of *wicking layers* (even long sleeve) in hot countries**

Thin layers of merino wool and some sporting synthetic fabrics has been shown to keep cool and help regulate core temperature.

PART 2: 1 DAY OTC PRACTICAL PERFORMANCE

This is usually evaluated on a one-day team activity. Occasionally it may be offered in two half days.
Candidate's Uniform and kit and clothing is checked right at the beginning of day one

LOCATION ____

NOTES	RESCUE ROPE BASICS	INITIAL	DATE

RESCUE ROPE BASICS

(These must be so comfortable they can be tied with gloves and almost blindfolded! If they candidate is struggling and getting it wrong, it is NOT a pass and it is a disservice to them and the team to do so, because when a proper knot is needed it may jeopardize member standards or even safety.)

(This is observed and signed off by an authorized senior member)

☐ **Can recite the 4 types of rope and examples of when used.**

1. KERNMANTLE: Static or Low Stretch for Rescue Rope

2. KERNMANTLE: Dynamic or High Stretch for climbing Rope

3. TWISTED LAID / HAWSER: Like manilla / boat rope

4. GP LINE: General Purpose Cordage / utility not rescue rope

☐ **Can dress a knot & finish the phrase: "*A neat knot is … *"**

"*A Happy Knot*" … meaning it looks neat and feels good and strong.

☐ **Can explain the different between a standard knot, bend and hitch.**

BEND: This knot connects two or more ropes

BITCH: Connects to an object. When removed knot comes undone

☐ **Can tie a Bowline**

NOTES

☐ **Can tie a Figure 8 on a bight (and a rethread Fig 8.)**

1   2   3   4

☐ **Can tie an Alpine Butterfly**

☐ **Can tie a Double Fisherman (stopper or connector / bend)**

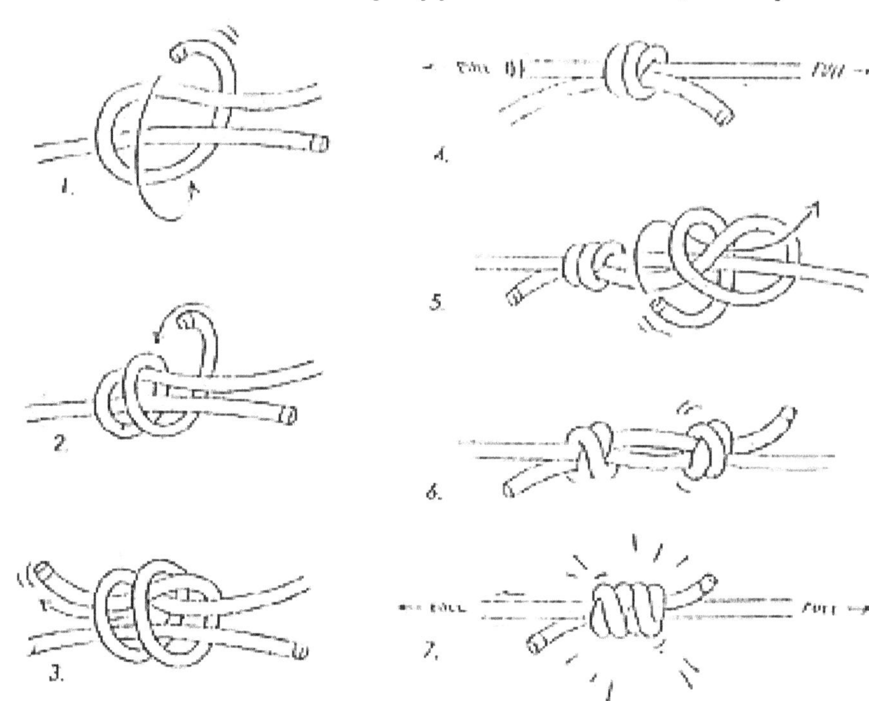

☐ **Can tie a round turn and two half hitches**

Round Turn With Two Half Hitches

☐ Can tie a Tensionless Hitch

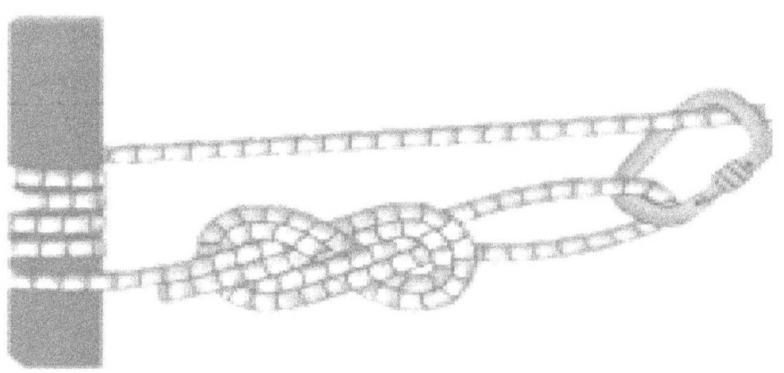

☐ **Can recognize a Mooring Hitch (and ideally proper OXO I Cleat Hitch)**

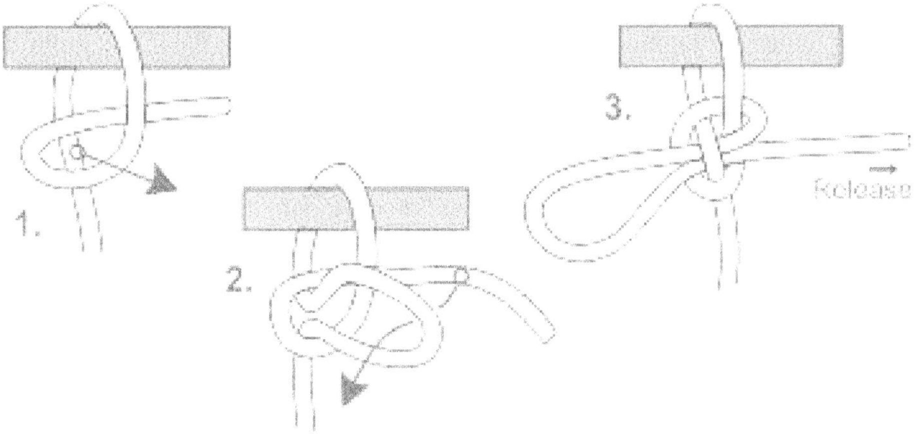

Mooring Hitch

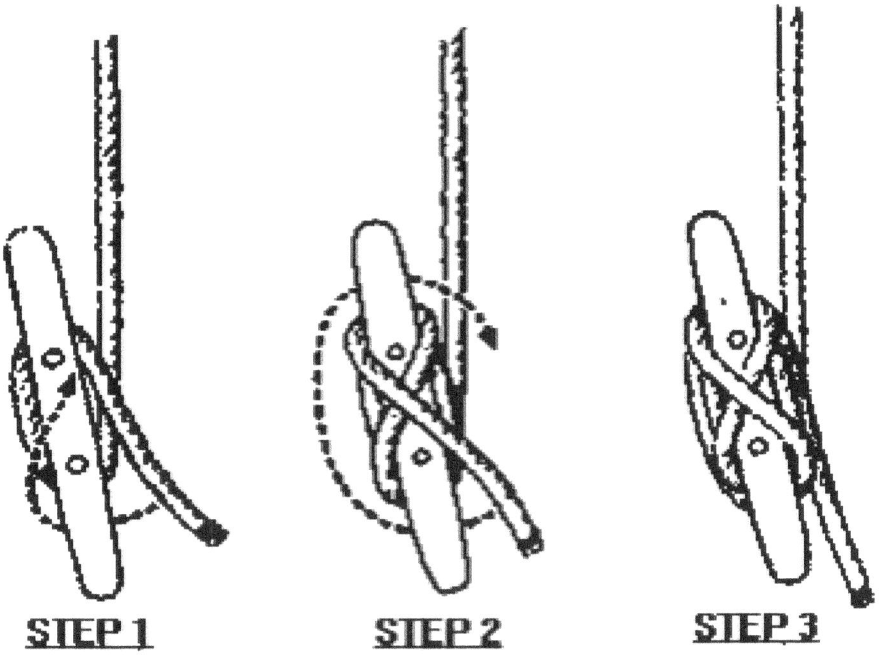

"OXO" Cleat Hitch

☐ **Can recite 3 ERT SAR Rope Rules / SOPs.**

1. Always carry a cutting instrument / knife (Often on a lanyard)

2. Do not STEP ON / STAND ON Rope

3. Do not Straddle rope – especially working line

4. Protect From Edges (with some form of "Edge Protection"

5. Protect from dirt, grit, chemicals, excess sun & clean when needed

☐ **Can explain why we don't "arm coil" a rope**

Often tangles and creates a "memory" not easy to throw or pay out

☐ **Can simple figure 8 coil a rope ("Flake")**

Figure 8 Flake

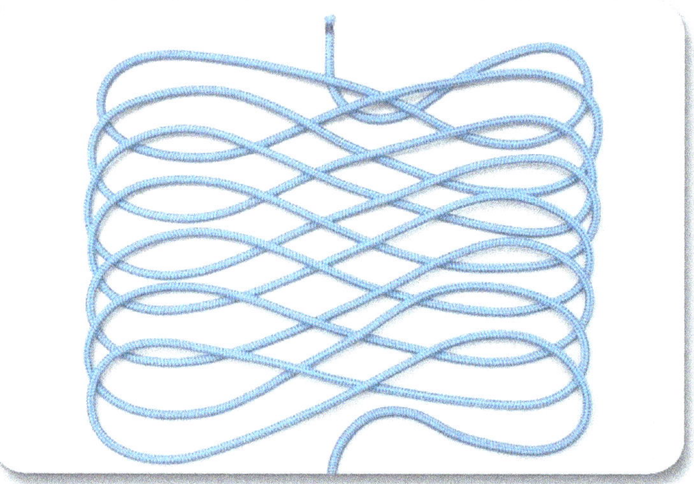

☐ **Knows what the purpose of "under over" (electricians' coil) of rope**

☐ Reduces tangling and pays out / springs better especially if thrown.

☐ **Can demonstrate 'hanking' paracord / cordage.**

☐ Figure 8 wind of cordage between thumb and little finger.

☐ **Can demonstrate daisy chaining coiling on a bight**

☐ This will be demonstrated by doing at least 4 to 5 consecutive loops

- *Other knots will be learned like Munter Hitch, Mooring Hitch etc.*
- *Munter hitch without a rope grab is not preferred for persons but should be perfectly acceptable for equipment.*

PART 2: 1 DAY OTC PRACTICAL PERFORMANCE

NOTES	WATER SAFETY & RESCUE	INITIAL	DATE

☐ **Can explain the orientation of the River left and right**

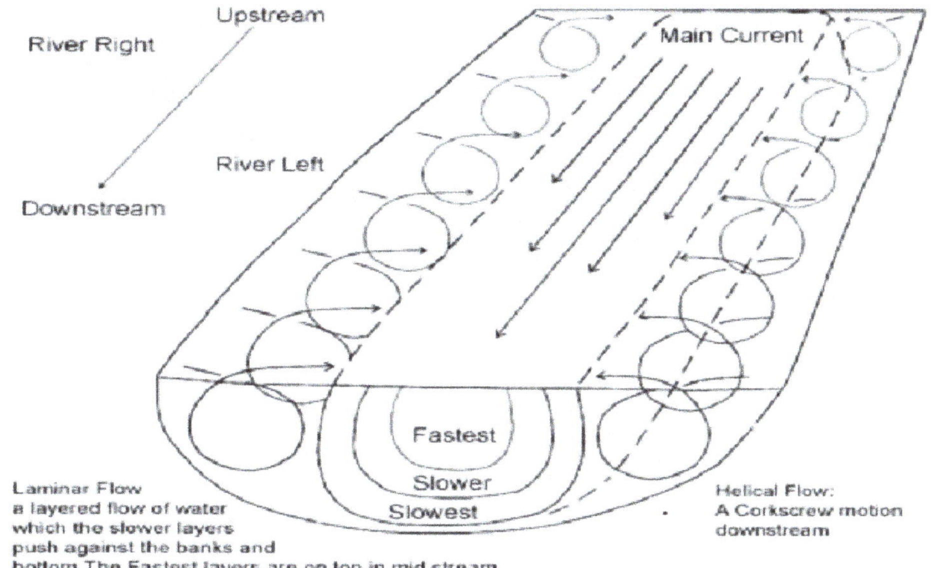

☐ **Can explain why searches on one bank also view the other**

Sometimes easier to see other side and harder to see yours

☐ **Can state the three main types of river water travel and movement**

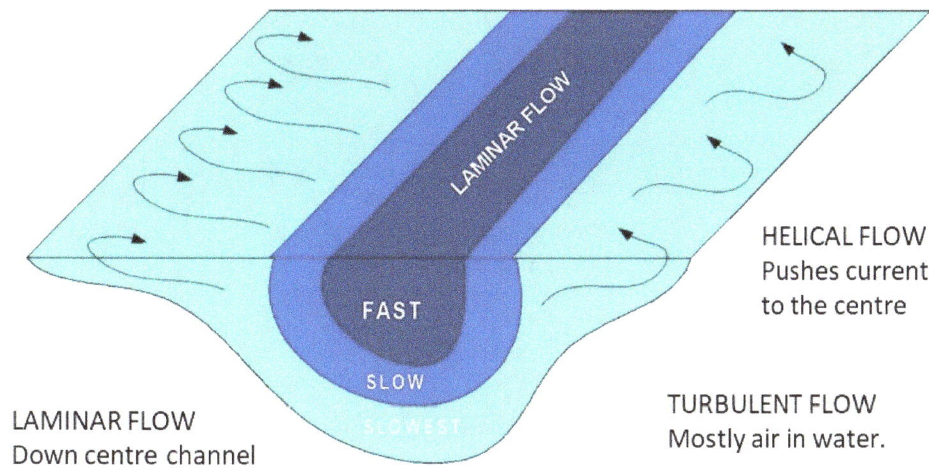

1.Lamnar Flow (down centre channel)

2. Helical Flow (corkscrewing the outside to the center and on)

3. Turbulent Flow (Aerated, fast moving White Water hitting objects)

☐ **Can recite the difference between a "Life Vest" and a "Rescuer PFD"**

☐ Lifevest "Rights your head" Manual vs Auto. PFD prob. better 4 Rescue

☐ **Knows the distance to wear a PFD on a bank with fast moving water**

Minimum 3 meters or 10 feet and in ALL Boats.

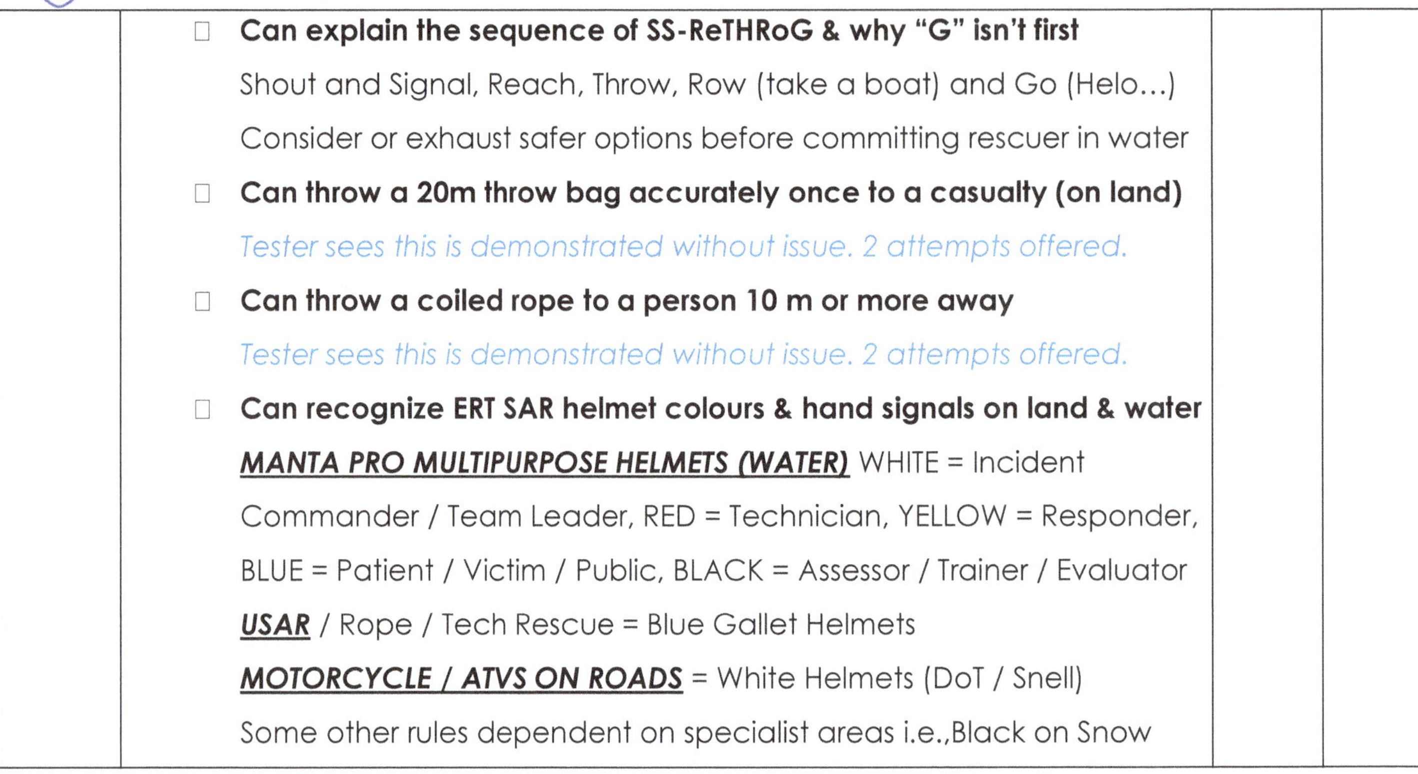

☐ **Can explain the sequence of SS-ReTHRoG & why "G" isn't first**

Shout and Signal, Reach, Throw, Row (take a boat) and Go (Helo…)

Consider or exhaust safer options before committing rescuer in water

☐ **Can throw a 20m throw bag accurately once to a casualty (on land)**

Tester sees this is demonstrated without issue. 2 attempts offered.

☐ **Can throw a coiled rope to a person 10 m or more away**

Tester sees this is demonstrated without issue. 2 attempts offered.

☐ **Can recognize ERT SAR helmet colours & hand signals on land & water**

MANTA PRO MULTIPURPOSE HELMETS (WATER) WHITE = Incident

Commander / Team Leader, RED = Technician, YELLOW = Responder,

BLUE = Patient / Victim / Public, BLACK = Assessor / Trainer / Evaluator

USAR / Rope / Tech Rescue = Blue Gallet Helmets

MOTORCYCLE / ATVS ON ROADS = White Helmets (DoT / Snell)

Some other rules dependent on specialist areas i.e.,Black on Snow

PART 2: 1 DAY OTC PRACTICAL PERFORMANCE

NOTES	CASUALTY RESPONSE, HANDING & MANAGEMENT	INITIAL	DATES

☐ **Has seen a Mass Casualty Triage Algorithm**

ERTSAR Tend to use "30:2 Can Do" for basic levels

The S.O.R.T. Triage is covered for more senior Triage Teams

<table>
<tr><td colspan="3" align="center">START Triage
Assess, *Treat*, *(use bystanders)*
When you have a color
STOP - TAG - MOVE ON</td></tr>
<tr><td rowspan="7">**M I N O R**</td><td colspan="2">-- *Move Walking Wounded*</td></tr>
<tr><td rowspan="6">**D E C E A S E D**</td><td colspan="2">-- No RESPIRATIONS after *head tilt*</td></tr>
<tr><td rowspan="5">**I M M E D I A T E**</td><td>-- **Breathing** but UNCONSCIOUS</td></tr>
<tr><td>-- **Respirations** - over 30</td></tr>
<tr><td>-- **Perfusion** Capillary refill > 2 or NO RADIAL PULSE
Control bleeding</td></tr>
<tr><td>-- **Mental Status** Unable to follow simple commands</td></tr>
<tr><td rowspan="2">**D E L A Y E D**</td><td>-- Otherwise</td></tr>
<tr><td>**REMEMBER:**

Respirations - 30
Perfusion - 2
Mental Status - Can Do</td></tr>
</table>

☐ **Can explain 3 challenges / pitfalls of (mass casualty) Triage**

Triage is required any time that the number of casualties outnumber the number of rescuers / medics. This is not always easy and there are many challenges and pitfalls which include:

1. Hesitation to perform it
2. Diffusion of responsibility (Someone else will do it)
3. No plan, No Organization, No Goal, No SOP,
4. No Training / Lack of understanding
5. No Triage Resources / No "Triage Kits" or adaptations
6. Indecisive Leadership at the time
7. It is mentally and emotionally difficult and very challenging
8. Performing Treatment versus Triage
9. Too much focus on one injury versus doing the most good
10. Lack of assistance in "Triage Teams" coordinating & helping

Remember Triage is often repeated and updated.

NOTES	

☐ **Can perform a rapid casualty *Response* using DR~~w~~s (C)ABCDE/SS**

☐ Depending who you talk to in which level of Medical response these letters mean different things but for now and in this context, they are:

- **D Danger Assessment/s**
- **R Responsiveness of Patient (AVPU)**
- ~~W – Has now been removed~~
- **S Shout for help**
- **(C) Catastrophic Bleeding**
- **A Airway**
- **B Breathing**
- **C Circulation**
- **D Defibrillation / Disability**
- **E Exposure / Everything else**
- **SS Secondary Survey and SAMPLE**

☐ **Is able to apply an Arm Tourniquet in a Catastrophic Haemorrhage**

This is observed and signed off by an authorized senior member
If they have a STOP THE BLEED CERTIFICATE or a TCCC Qualification or a Tactical Paramedic or similar this may be waived and signed off

☐ **Is able to apply a Leg Tourniquet in a Catastrophic Haemorrhage**

This is observed and signed off by an authorized senior member
If they have a STOP THE BLEED CERTIFICATE or a TCCC Qualification or a Tactical Paramedic or similar this may be waived and signed off

☐ **Understands how to perform wound packing technique on *Cat Hem***

This is observed and signed off by an authorized senior member
If they have a STOP THE BLEED CERTIFICATE or a TCCC Qualification or a Tactical Paramedic or similar this may be waived and signed off

☐ **Can articulate the manual handling lifting in words and directions**

Not 1, 2, 3 lift (or similar) but using the WORDS, "READY?...." Await recognition "BRACE" (give the instruction to lifting / moving team) and then "ACTION" Word, for example "LIFT" or "LOWER" or "MOVE" etc.

☐ **Shows good kinetic lifting & manual handling technique**

Using Acronym B.A.C.K. they should remember to be strong and balanced standing close as possible to object and lifting with Legs (not arms and back) per se. The Acronym BACK is often used thus:

Balanced with strong steady footing and close to object

Alignment meaning usually not awkward twisting of spine with arms away from body

Closeness to object (Don't "reach" and bear weight only in transition)

Knees bent and use your leg muscles to lift

☐ **Opens a folding stretcher and lifts and packages a casualty onto it**
This is observed and signed off by an authorized senior member
It is usually done as a pair but can be done individually.

☐ **Can lift & move litter / stretcher as a team on flat ground**
This is observed and signed off by an authorized senior member
"Ready Brace & Lift "and good manual handling and communication with Feet First down sustained heavy inclines (So patient does not have blood rushing to the head). Method is to WALK with strong grip

☐ **Can lift & move litter / stretcher as a team on hilly / undulating ground**
This is observed and signed off by an authorized senior member
"Ready Brace & Lift "and good manual handling and communication with Feet First down sustained heavy inclines (So patient does not have blood rushing to the head). Method is to PASS HAND TO HAND and then WALK to the end and take over. NOT walking. (Catepillar)

☐ **Completes 3 team casualty carries (can be completed after fitness)**

☐ SINGLE PERSON: Human Crutch, Pack Strap Carry, Fireman's Carry, Drags and Firefighter's Crawl

☐ TWO RESCUER: Chair Lift, Two Hand Seat Cary, Three Hand (Assisted Support) Carry, Four Hand Seat carry, Blanket / Stretcher Carry, etc.

☐ MULTI-RESCUER: Many options such as Tactical Carry, Stretcher etc

☐ **Can use rigid and soft (sheet) stretchers and drag harnesses**

☐ Demonstrated. Eh Foxtrot Litter. Pictures will illustrate.

☐ **Can complete a medical patient report form (usually the PRF – Lite)**
ERT SAR uses 3 main 'paper forms' and also support some ePRFs.

PRF - *Lite*

AMBULANCE HANDOVER: Y / N
WHO TO:

ERT SAR.com – Patient Report Form (Lite)

www.ERT-SAR.com   HQ@ERT-SAR.com   *To be completed before handover / file*

DATE ___________ TIME _________ OFFICER:___________

PATIENT NAME ___________________________________

DOB (dd/mm/yy)_____________ AGE: _____ SEX: M / F

TEL:__________________(Mob / H / W)

ADDRESS_______________________________

WITNESS: _______________________

TEL:________________ WHO_________

☐ O2   ☐ N2O2   ☐ CPR   ☐ DEFIB

SIGNS/SYMPTOMS_______________________________

ANY ALLERGIES___________MEDICATION____________

PERTINENT HISTORY ______________________________

LAST ORAL INTAKE_______________________________

Hx INJURY OR ILLNESS ____________________________

TREATMENT SO FAR?______________________________

Time

1 BLOOD PRESSURE ____ /_____ HEART RATE ____bpm
O2 SATS ______ BLOOD SUGAR _______ PUPILS______

Time

2 BLOOD PRESSURE ____ /_____ HEART RATE ____bpm
O2 SATS ______ BLOOD SUGAR _______ PUPILS______

NOTE: If you use ANY Medications including Oxygen (O2) and Entonox (N2O2) please RECORD IT. And then

PART 2: 1 DAY OTC PRACTICAL PERFORMANCE

NOTES	TEAM FITNESS (BFT Plus) & NAVIGATION EXERCISE	INITIAL	DATE

NOTE: The Fitness Test has a required set up and can be done with a Nav-Ex

The testers / invigilators need to make a request to complete an official test as the date and weather conditions are recorded 'in the book" and usually there needs to be TWO qualified Seniors 'running' the test with a 'Safety' and this is all explained in the "ERT SAR Fitness Test Guidelines." There are a few different "Fitness Tests" but the standard one for all members is the enhanced 5 mile walk in 2 hours in uniform belt kit and the sprint & calisthenics etc. at the end. (This is usually done on the annual fitness test, OTC weekend or specially designated fitness session. Enhanced version is preferred for all C & D Squad including Marine Unit. Minimum Basic is acceptable for B Squad.)

Fitness is important in ERT SAR as is operational capacity. Injuries and problems can arise from unhealthy and obese candidates. We care little for other BMIs.

☐ Pass **BMI standard of 30** or less RESULT: WT______ HT______ BMI ______ * *

1. ~~28 is optimum (like Marines) for the Challenge Coin unless muscled~~
2. The regular for rescuers is 30 BMI unless heavily muscled.
3. The operational standard norm is "proportionate Height & Weight" and fit for duty, able to pass the enhanced fitness test.

☐ **RESULT:**   PASS | FAILL | ADVISORY ______________________ * *

☐ **Time completed the enhanced Fitness Test (not Basic):** ___________

☐ *This is observed and signed off by an authorized senior member*

☐ **Push ups, sit ups and standing / sit is completed right at the time.**

☐ *This is observed and signed off by an authorized senior member*

☐ **Can *Farmer Carry* half their own weight over 100 feet in 2 minutes * ***

☐ *This is observed and signed off by an authorized senior member*

☐ **Maintains a regimen of physical activity. e.g.** _____________________

☐ *This is stated and with some 'validation' to the Senior Member*

☐ **Performed Team Navigation exercise 5 miles in 90 to 120 minutes.**

☐ *This is observed and signed off by an authorized senior member * **

☐ **Successfully completes NAVEX as a functioning Member of a team**

☐ *This is observed and signed off by an authorized senior member*

☐ **Can calculate relative time zone / hours based on lat / long**

☐ *This is demonstrated based on the 15 Deg per one hour standard*

☐ **Knows the Cardinal Points of a Compass and at which degree**

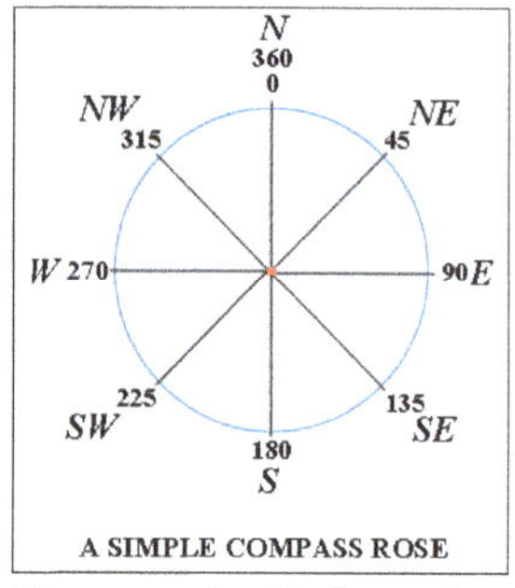

This is checked twice by an authorized senior member by giving a "Cardinal Point" and getting a Degree Bearing or offering a "Bearing and getting a "Cardinal Point" in which these equates to NORTH = 0 Deg, EAST = 90 Deg, SOUTH = 180 Deg & WEST = 270 Deg.

☐ **Can calculate a back bearing from a forward bearing**

☐ *This is checked twice by an authorized senior member on the 180 Deg Rule i.e., if you go out on 270 Deg then you come back on 90 Deg.*

☐ **Knows the three different "Norths" and their relevance**

☐ Candidate will be asked about the three main "Norths" These will be 1. True North, 2. Grid North and 3. Magnetic North. (Some say there is a 4[th] = Google Maps North.)

<u>1. True North</u> on a map is the direction of a line of longitude which converges on the North Pole. <u>2. Grid North</u> The grid lines of a map point to a Grid North, varying slightly from True North. This happens because a "Globe" is transferred to a flat map for reference / reading. The difference between grid north and true north is very small on most maps especially away from the poles. and for most navigation purposes can almost always be negated (unless at the edges / near the poles. <u>3. Magnetic North</u> compass needle points to the 3rd North which is the "magnetic" north pole. The horizontal angular difference between True North and Magnetic North is called MAGNETIC VARIATION or DECLINATION and it is more important the closer to the North Pole and when high accuracy is important.

☐ **Knows where the Prime Meridian is located & where is *Intl Date Line***

☐ **This is observed and signed off by an authorized senior member**

**Unless heavily muscled. This matches the Officer standard in the Royal Marines.*

*** Some discrepancy upon appeal but all operational members need to aim for this*

PART 2: 1 DAY OTC PRACTICAL PERFORMANCE

NOTES	TEAM GROUP EXERCISE/S	INITIAL	DATES

☐ **Carries fire making item/s and can start a survival Fire _(May not test)_**

Carries flint striker, magnesium rod and windproof lighter or waterproof survival matches. It is desired to make and keep a fire going.

☐ **Demonstration of the "(Foo) Dirty Mapping" method**

Draw a rough but clear paper map of the area as taught with North on the map, routes, places / buildings, resources (water, toilets, LX) and Hazards and relate to the disaster or incident.

☐ **Completes a Ground Search Exercise without being distracted**

Given an exercise to find a missing or lost person / persons that needs to be found, that they look using the "Search Cube" (left, right, up. down, forward and back and all around). They look, search and recognize what's needed and do not operate distracted. When searching with others they do not 'chat' and forget the purpose of the search. Doesn't walk in large group of several members. (Below)

☐ **Is not "Swarming" (walking in crowded group) chatting during search.**

Candidates are testing over at least 10 to 15 minutes. Real person searches of persons (not usually known) often used for this portion.

PART 3: FOUNDATION KNOWLEDGE

NOTES	SAFETY AND SECURITY INTRODUCTION	INITIAL	DATE

☐ **Knows *"The Number One Rule of Rescue"* and why?**

"Safety of the Rescuer"… Rescuer/s should not also need rescue!

☐ **Can recite the "Firefighters" / "Rescuers" Creed.**

☐ The phrase or creed is: "We take measured risk to save a life but we do not take risk to save the lost or property."

☐ **Self-Rescue and Buddy Rescue Concepts**

"Self-Rescue" is the being able to take oneself (or group) out of a hazardous or compromised situation, using their knowledge, skills and probably kit without the need for external assistance (usually). *"Buddy Rescue Concepts"* implies working with another person who is instrumental in assisting or supporting the rescue. For example they may simply catch a rope thrown to them over a ravine or water or more instrumentally, participate in essential components of the rescue, or simply act as another person and safety person.

☐ **The importance of Communication and working in Pairs**

Working in pairs can make you more efficient to get tasks done Working in pairs offers a safety and security support and communication is vital to information sharing and objectives.

☐ **Why freelancing is usually discouraged & PAS is important**

PAS is "Personal Accountability System" or "Tallies" (UK) and this involves knowing WHO you have got working WHERE and WHAT they are doing. Freelancing implies that the member has *"gone off script"* and is leaving the scope of "Direction" and "SOPs" and usually implies doing their own thing. Even worse, often without telling Leadership where they gone and asked if they could. Therefore, their efforts may be potentially unsafe and activities unknown to the rest of the team, which is not desired.

☐ **What is a RIT / RIC Function and why we do it in training?**

"RIT / RIC" stands for Rapid Intervention Team or Rapid Intervention Crew and these are usually a small team of specialists who are designated to respond to an incident and rescue a rescuer, or a fellow team member who has got in trouble, during the incident.

☐ **Candidate understands why they should be 'security aware'**

Safety is the number one rule of rescue. Rescuers may be exposed to threats including human and natural threats.

☐ **Understands what is "Situational Awareness" (SA)**

This is continuously using all your senses with training, experience and a heightened sense of awareness in the environment, and making adaptations to maintain safety & manage hazards & risks.

☐ **Knows the *Coopers Colour Codes***

Jeff Cooper's was a former US Marine who developed a an Awareness Color Code Chart. The late Jeff Cooper's "Color Code" as a mental process for breaking down alertness levels into four colors: White, Yellow, Orange and Red. Later black was added.

White	Unprepared and unready to take action.
Yellow	Prepared, alert & relaxed. Good situational awareness.
Orange	Alert to probable danger. Ready to take action.
Red	Action Mode. Focused on the emergency at hand.
Black	Panic. Breakdown of physical & mental performance.

☐ *Condition White* represents a state of complete unawareness and unpreparedness. *Condition Yellow* represents a state of relaxed alert. There is no specific, obvious threat present, but you are aware that danger is always a possibility. You are aware of people around you as well as the environment in general. *Condition Orange*. This is a heightened state of awareness in which you observe or are aware of a specific threat and READY to take Action. In this condition, you are beginning to formulate possible responses to deal with the danger. *Condition Red* is the stage associated with action. *Condition Black* (was added later) is usually "Panic" and (undesired) loss of control.

☐ **Understanding threat and risk profiles**

☐ Common types of physical security threats include *Assault, Theft & Burglary Vandalism, Sabotage, Terrorism & Disasters*. Risk needs to be controlled with preparedness and mitigation to your exposure.,

☐ **Using layers for protection**

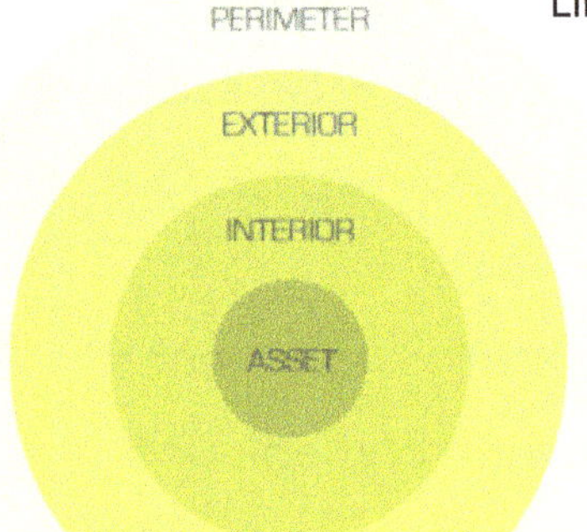

Like Layers of an Onion, this approach is common to physical security threats and vulnerabilities. Exterior: Access control procedures & security measures mitigate most attempts. Interior: Reinforcement use intelligent countermeasures against more determined and professionals' attempts. Asset: Internal enclosures fortified against extreme attack with emergency lockdown and rapid response.

☐ **Performing Size-Ups and Risk Assessments**

Constant DRA (Dynamic Risk Assessments) know the risks, watch and monitor the issues. i.e., a Collapsed structure, watch for cracks, listen for creaking, cracks, hissing (gas), running water, etc., Size ups are constant and always performed before any operation, on arrival and during the operation.

PART 3: FOUNDATION KNOWLEDGE

NOTES	**DISASTER RESPONSE BASICS** *Obviously if using this sheet do not show the answers. Ask and check answer.*	INITIAL	DATE

☐ **Candidate can list the three (3) Main types of Disaster**

Most disaster specialists remind people that 'all' disasters' are actually

(Hu)Man Made and also remember that there is a difference

between Disasters and "Hazards". The 3 types are

1. Natural such as Earthquake and Storms

2. Man-Made such as Terrorism

3. Technological such as Power Cuts

☐ **Understands the concepts of the Disaster Management Cycle**

1. Preparedness | 2. Response | 3. Recovery | 4. Mitigation

What is Disaster Management?

Preparedness -- activities prior to a disaster.
Examples: preparedness plans; emergency
exercises/training; warning systems.

Response -- activities during a disaster.
Examples: public warning systems;
emergency operations; search and
rescue.

Recovery -- activities following a disaster.
Examples: temporary housing; claims
processing and grants; long-term medical
care and counseling.

Mitigation - activities that reduce the effects of
disasters.
Examples: building codes and zoning; vulnerability
analyses; public education.

☐ **Can explain how ERT SAR aids in Surge Capacity**

Basically, Surge capacity is used in medical and healthcare circles

when a sudden influx of patients push the ability to accommodate a

significant increase in patients. In disaster and humanitarian affairs it

reflects when there are unforeseen emergencies and disasters, when

a crisis deteriorates, or when a force majeure affects an ability to

respond under usual and normal operational capacity.

Medical surge capacity refers to the ability to evaluate and care for a markedly increased volume of patients—one that challenges or exceeds normal operating capacity. The surge requirements may extend beyond direct patient care to include such tasks as extensive laboratory studies or epidemiological investigations.

☐ **Has watched the ERT SAR video: "Aerial Disaster Assessments"**

☐ The video is on Youtube. Also www.ERT-SAR.com/helicopter-training & the tester must *signed off as an authorized senior member*

☐ **Can recall 3 things needed to perform this, from video.**

The tester will ask three questions and if satisfied then they *will sign off as this portion as an authorized senior member.*

☐ **Knows what is the "(Foo) Dirty Mapping" method**

This is where you draw a rough but clear paper map (or occasionally digital map) of the area. The N with an arrow is inserted with North on the map. Any roads, rivers, lakes, paths, routes as well as structures / places / buildings and any resources (water, toilets, LX) and Hazards. This 'dirty map' should be related to the disaster or incident. Also note that a picture can be taken and layered over the 'top' of a google Map KML / KMZ file to update the environment and conditions.

PART 3: FOUNDATION KNOWLEDGE

NOTES	SAR (SEARCH AND RESCUE) ACRONYMS & SURVIVAL MNEMONICS	INITIAL	DATE

☐ **Can recite the L.A.S.T. acronym and what it means in SAR**

☐ In SAR = Locate, Access, Stabilise, Transport. There are 3 types of Stabilisation (according to CMC) 1) Physical, Mental and Medical.

☐ **Understand the 3 types of *Active Search* with example**

- *Type I* = Hasty (UK) | Initial Response / Initial Sweep (USA & Canada)
- *Type II* = Efficient (UK) | Sweep Search / Open Grid (USA & Canada)
- *Type III* = Thorough (UK) | Closed Grid (USA & Canada)

  (Also good to have Mantrackers | SAR Dog | MBSAR)

☐ **Understand the 3 types of *Passive Search* with example**

Passive Searching involves making the lost of missing come to you, containing the areas and using 'magnets' to attract them. "Magnets" can be broken down into 3 categories with the letters P, A, and N.

P = Personal. i.e., Shops, areas of personal interest or nostalgia, etc.

A = Artificial. i.e., Towns, City Centres, Lights, Sirens, Music Playing,

N = Natural. i.e., Natural beauty, Scenic Views, Cliffs, Water Features,

☐ **Can recite the Three main "Survival Law / Rule of Threes"**

Survival Law of 3's that expresses when these items are compromised your health or life may be in danger. In order of priority these are:

- *3 Minutes without Air*
- *3 Days without Water*
- *3 Weeks without Food And some say …*
- *(3 hours without shelter" in a harsh or extreme environment.*
- *3 Months without Company.)*

☐ **Can articulate the meaning of the S.T.O.P.-P.**

☐ Upon checking they can recite **S**top, **T**hink, **O**bserve, **P**lan - **P**roceed

☐ **Can articulate the meaning of P.L.A.N.-M. in survival**

☐ *Protection* from the environment (Clothing, Footwear, PPE, Shelter, fire making and lighting.)

☐ *Location* = close enough to supplies and area needed (shelter, food, water area, close to helicopter extraction, signal fire etc.) But away from close hazards (like wild animals or incoming tide on a beach) and also includes being seen and being able to signal;

☐ *Acquisition* means getting hold of needed items starting with Water and food – as well as other needed resources. This may mean making tools or sourcing materials to fix your equipment;

☐ *Navigation* by whatever means are available;

☐ *Medical* including health and welfare. Lok after yourself, self rescue through treatment and recognition of developing conditions you don't want to worsen (such as blisters) and using your first-aid knowledge in combination with available or improvised materials.

☐ **Can list at least 6 types of SAR or Technical Rescue disciplines**

This are mostly the Technical Rescue Disciplines of the NFPA 1006 and similar such as: *ROPE RESCUE* (One of the primary subjects) and also (The items in bold are most common and often used in C Squad)

• Tower Rescue	• Machinery RSQ	• **USAR/Structural Collapse**
• Vehicle Rescue	• Helicopter RSQ	• Confined Space Rescue
• Trench Rescue	• Dive Rescue	• Mine & Tunnel Rescue
• Surf Recue	• Ice Rescue	• **Swiftwater Rescue**
• **Wilderness SAR**	• **Surface water &**	• **Floodwater Rescue**
• Cave Rescue	• **Watercraft RSQ**	• Animal Tech Rescue
• Wildland Fire	• Bushfirefighter	• Mud Rescue

PART 3: FOUNDATION KNOWLEDGE

NOTES	ONLINE LEARNING COURSES	INITIAL	DATES
	It is recommended the applicant/Candidate completes supporting training ☐ **Completed ERT SAR Uniform Module** bit.ly/ERTUNIFORM *Certificate seen so this can be signed off by an authorized senior* ☐ **Completed ERT SAR Kit and Equipment Module** bit.ly/ERTKIT1 *Certificate seen so this can be signed off by an authorized senior* ☐ **Completes *Ground Search & Rescue* Course (online)** bit.ly/ERTGSAR1 *Certificate seen so this can be signed off by an authorized senior* ☐ **Completes *Helicopter Safety & Formations* Course online/face to face** *Certificate seen (TBC) so this can be signed off by authorized senior*		

PART 3: FOUNDATION KNOWLEDGE

NOTES	FINAL ATTENDANCE CHECKS & SEEN DOCUMENTS (Check & date when shown)	INITIAL	DATES

☐ **Has reviewed GSMEAC *Briefing* Document Example & can recite**

Briefing Aide Memoire. Points listed in summary sheet below.

☐ **Has reviewed (Foo) *"Flow cycle aide memoire"* for GSAR / Operations**

www.ERT-SAR.com　　info@ERT-SAR.com　　Copyright 2008 Gary Foo Revised 2020 V20

SAR FLOW CYCLE & AIDE MEMOIRE

DISASTER: NATURAL, MAN MADE or SAR

Debriefing
(Reverse SMEAC)

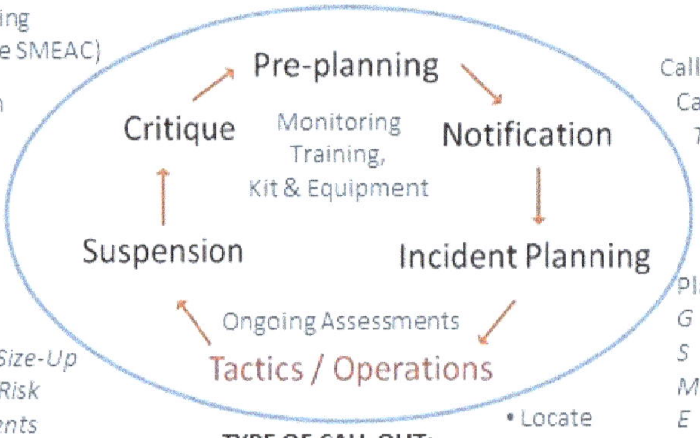

Collate Information
Demobilization
Stand Down

SCORPA
Size up
Contingencies
Objectives
Resources
Plan
Action.

*Safety & Size-Up
Dynamic Risk
Assessments
Health & Safety
SPC: Safe Person Concept*

Flow cycle (inner circle): Pre-planning → Notification → Incident Planning → Tactics / Operations → (Ongoing Assessments) → Suspension → Critique → Pre-planning. Monitoring Training, Kit & Equipment (centre).

NOTIFICATION
Call in: PLB, Phone call, Absent, etc
Call Out: "Shout" | Deployment
Text / WhatsApp / TeamApp
(Initiate "Overhead Team")
How to manage Incident
BRIEFING

Planned: GSMEAC
G　Ground　　GOLD: Strategic
S　Situation　SILVER: Tactical
M　Mission　　BRONZE: Operational
E　Execution
A　Admin / Logistics
C　Command / Communications

TYPE OF CALL OUT:
Disaster? Missing / Lost?

MEETING POINTS
RVP　　Rendez-Vous Point
FOB　　Forward Operating Base
SHA　　Strategic holding area
MASHA　Multi-Agency Strategic Holding
Area
ICP　　Incident Command Point

• Locate
• Access
• Stabilise
 - Emotional
 - Medical
 - Physical
 Transport

Emergency: STICC
S Here's what we face
T Here's what I think we should do
I Here's Why
C Here's what we should watch
C Now, talk to me…

M　My Call Sign
E　Exact Location
T　Type of Incident
H　Hazards (Present / Potential)
A　Access (to scene)
N　Number of casualties & type
E　Emergency Services (here & Needed)

Leadership & Management
1 Safety
2 Mission Achievement / Objective
3 Ensure Standards

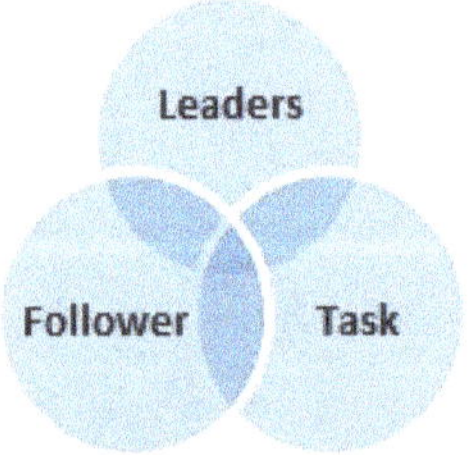

Leaders / Follower / Task

C　Command
S　Safety
C　Communication
A　Assessment
T　Triage
T　Treatment
T　Transport

C　Catastrophic Compressible Haemorrhage
A　Airway
B　Breathing
C　Circulation
D　Disability
E　Exposure

MIST Handover
• Mechanism
• Injury
• Signs
• Treatment

SAD CHALETS
scene management:
S Survey
A Assess
D Disseminate

C Casualties
H Hazards
A Access
L Location
E Emergency
Services
T Type of incident
S Start a log

FOO's 5 MISSING / LOST
1. Lost
2. Missing
3. Abducted
4. Seized
5. Absent

*Emergencies: STOPp
Survival Rule of 3s
6 Survival Needs
Clothing (3 Ws)
Navigation: map & Compass
Equipment & Vehicles & PPE
Composition & Communication*

RESCUE RELIEF
(Body *Recovery*)
Helo
Ropes
Height
Water / Intl. / DEFRA
Fire
USAR
Terrorism
Haz-Mat
Emergencies
Hazards
Disasters
And so forth?...

LEADERSHIP & SAFETY
Team Composition

COMMUNICATION
Skills & Technqs

REPORTS
Status Rep.
Sit-Rep
Welfare Check

MEDICAL NEEDS

Establish Search Area
•Theoretical
•Statistical
•Subjective
•Deductive Reasoning

PASSIVE
•Track Traps
•Confinement
•Magnets (P.A.N.)
•Attraction etc.

Casualty? Clues? Management of Evidence

Lost Person Behaviour
•Profiling
•Investigating
•Planning
•Operations

ACTIVE
• Type I
• Type II
• Type III
• Specialist…

ASSETS
Dogs
Horses
Bikes
(Hu)Man Trackers, etc

MARCHE
Protocol

The Use of Drones
Seeing Vs. Searching
Advanced: Night & Low Light

NOTES	

☐ **Has reviewed *"Pre-event check list"*, *(& has link to online version)***

Printed version available.

Online Version here: http://bit.ly/PREEVENTERTSAR

☐ **Has reviewed a *"Triage algorithm"* or done the course:** bit.ly/ERTTriage

The "30:2 Can" method is the standard. **The S.A.L.T. Method** is expected by more senior medics. **S.A.L.T.** is an acronym for Sort, Assess, Life-saving interventions, Treatment and/or Transport) Triage

☐ **Has reviewed the 3 types of medical *"PRF"* (Patient Report Form.)**

The Regular PRF Lite was shown earlier in this document.

There is also a (modified or not) TCCC card used for for disasters *EQs* (Earthquakes etc) and finally a long form (Ambulance) Patient Report Form *(PRF)* usually used by Pre-Hospital Emergency Care (PHEC) environments and more serious incidents where there is time and need to use the long form – if available. The version below is TCCC.

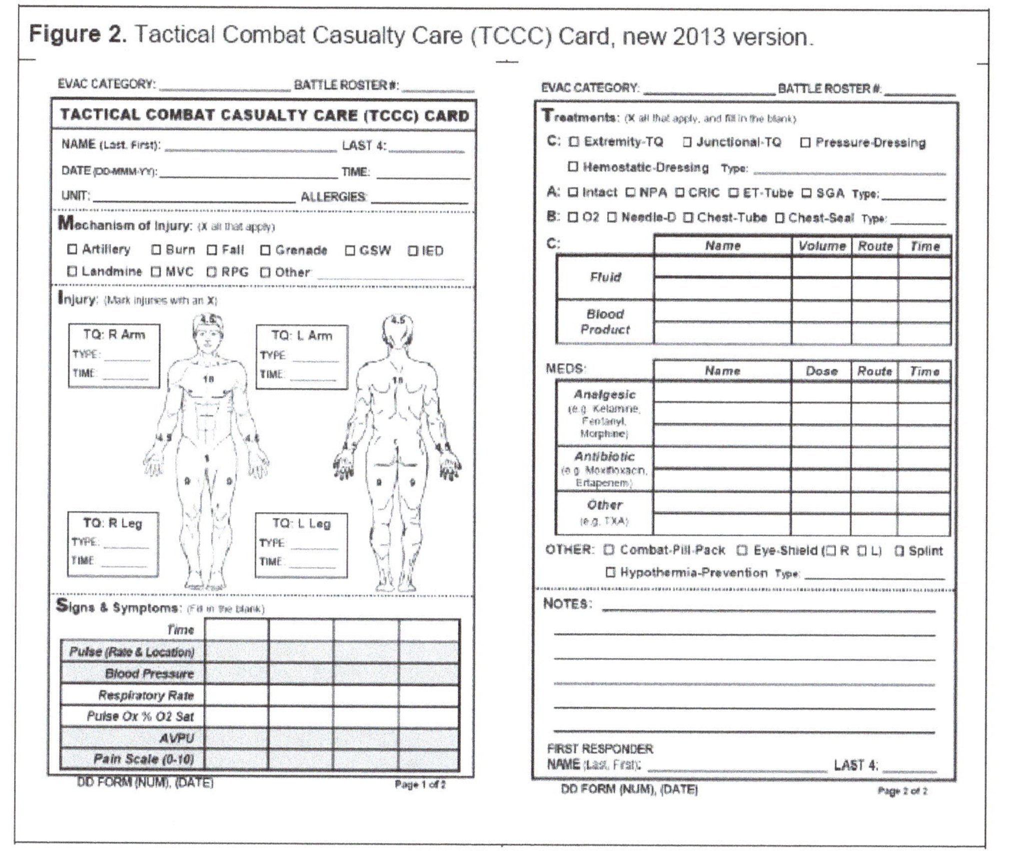

Figure 2. Tactical Combat Casualty Care (TCCC) Card, new 2013 version.

- ☐ **Has reviewed the *Flood Response Summary Sheet***
- ☐ Until 2021 this step will be waived in lieu of the explanation that the SDR (Safe Distance Reporting) is paramount and operational team members will be aware that the use of these practices and check sheets. SDR or Safe Distance Reporting is what ERT SAR do when we enter a hazard zone and should not or cannot easily write. This is often done by F.A.S.T. (Flood and Swiftwater Technical Teams) when doing do to door in flood environments. They report on radio and someone outside the cordon usually records or checks off the details and notes. It also happens in hazard zones and those "Hot-Zones" needing PPE.
- ☐ **Knows of Convoy Driving & Motorcycle / Motor Vehicle Standards**
  TO BE ADDED – Is in printed documents. May be online.
- ☐ **Completed the min. number of sessions (10 or 5, if fast tracked.)**
  (Fast Tracked candidates are unusual but usually medical doctors or with extensive complementary background or returning full members
- ☐ ***Add***
- ☐ **Candidate has attendance in all 4 areas including Training, eLearning (Online), Event and Exercise or Call Out. (Meeting not required)**
  Use TeamApp and Member Logs as evidence to support.
- ☐ **Candidate has done at least one or more "Events" in past 12 Months**
- ☐ One is a minimum for Operational Capacity. If H.E.A.T. Team (Primary) or Secondary, we would expect significantly more to show on record. That being said, there are not a lot of events so adjustments made,

Candidate should be awarded MEMBER Status and can access following items
- ✓ Certificate of successful completion showing join and completion date
- ✓ Wallet Certification Card showing join and completion date
- ✓ ERT SAR Operational Member Polo Shirt
- ✓ ERT SAR Member ID Card (PAS (Personal Accountability) in some cases.
- ✓ ERT SAR Line 2 "Operator" Challenge Coin
- ✓ Entered on *NEW* ERTSAR Register of SAR Operators and Humanitarians

PART 3: FOUNDATION KNOWLEDGE

NOTES	**WHAT'S NEXT** (Read this to Candidate. Initial any already done. Tick ones wanted)	INITIAL	DATES
	Candidate informed they can attend next Foundation Course. Which one/s?		
	☐ **Marine Unit Proficiency Levels 1 to 3 (or equivalency)**		
	☐ Level 1		
	☐ Level 2		
	☐ Level 3		
	☐ **Marine Unit Membership after MUP**		
	☐ Full or Applicant Status (but NOT Mandatory)		
	☐ **STC: Phase 3 – Specialist Training Course**		
	☐ _Details to be added as per SOPS_		
	☐ **ITC: Phase 4 – International Training Course**		
	☐ _Details to be added as per SOPS_		
	☐ **LTC: Phase 5 – Leadership Training Course**		
	☐ _Details to be added as per SOPS_		
	This does not have to be full to complete this. Just awareness of~		

PART 4: FINAL UNIFORM & KIT CHECK

NOTES	**UNIFORM INSPECTION:** Pass 3 Uniform Inspections (on 3 different days)	INITIAL & DATE	INITIAL & DATE	INITIAL & DATE

☐ <u>**Polished full black boots.**</u> **No coloured stitching. Laces not hanging. Not slip ons. Does not need to be steel toed. Black polished leather.**

(This is checked and signed off by an authorized senior member) ONE of these checks the boots may be a second "A" Boot not worn (NW) and pulled out for the day (if training outdoors) but member must describe how they polished the boots. The other 2 must be worn.

☐ **A *BONUS MARK* for bulled or highly polished cap of boots**

This is observed and signed off by an authorized senior member

☐ **Clean and pressed navy-blue trousers with cargo pockets**

This is observed and signed off by an authorized senior member

☐ **Black Belt & silver or plain buckle (not Rescuers riggers belt unless ~)**

This is observed and signed off by an authorized senior member

☐ **Blue Round Neck ERT SAR GUARDIAN Shirt / Polo Shirt <u>w/ Badges on</u>**

This is observed and signed off by an authorized senior member

☐ **Black long or short sleeved round neck wicking shirt underneath**

This is observed and signed off by an authorized senior member

☐ **Men shaved or neatly groomed beard. Ladies long hair tied back.**

This is observed and signed off by an authorized senior member

☐ **Candidate is clean, smart and neatly groomed.**

This is observed and signed off by an authorized senior member

☐ **Flags on uniform & knows which side respective collar dogs go on shirt**

This is observed and signed off by an authorized senior member

1 PRINT NAME OF LEADER, DATED & ANY MORE NOTES

____

2 PRINT NAME OF LEADER, DATED & ANY MORE NOTES

____

3 PRINT NAME OF LEADER, DATED & ANY MORE NOTES

____

NOTES: Simple summary below. Detailed inspection summary in Matrix & SOP Manual

PART 4: FINAL UNIFORM & KIT CHECK

NOTES	**GRAB BAG** (Grab bag has name on & country flag) **& upon inspection has**	INITIAL	DATE
	☐ *Food and snacks* *		
	☐ *This is observed and signed off by an authorized senior member*		
	☐ *Water* (2 to 4 litres) *		
	This is observed and signed off by an authorized senior member		
	☐ Small Personal *First Aid / Medical kit* *		
	This is observed and signed off by an authorized senior member		
	☐ *Some PPE* (like ear plugs, eye protection, face mask & nitrile gloves)		
	This is observed and signed off by an authorized senior member		
	☐ Own a pair of Riggers / Rescue style **Gloves**		
	This is observed and signed off by an authorized senior member		
	☐ Owns a Candidate **Coat** / Softshell jacket (& brings to every session) *		
	This is observed and signed off by an authorized senior member		
	☐ Small bag / pack for **Uniform Jacket** to fold into		
	This is observed and signed off by an authorized senior member		
	☐ Has a few extra kit supplies as per, **Mission Profile**		
	This is observed and signed off by an authorized senior member		
	☐ Some components of a **G1098 Kit**		
	This is observed and signed off by an authorized senior member		
	☐ Wet weather rucksack cover: black or yellow. (Contractor Garbage bag OK)		
	This is observed and signed off by an authorized senior member		
	☐ Has read a copy of the equipment and kit packing standards / SOPs		
	This is observed and signed off by an authorized senior member		
	NOTES: The items with an asterisk are mandatory and must be possessed by the Candidate in order to pass this inspection. Inverse Pyramid Packing & 10 rules for rules read from ERTSAR SOP manual.		

NOTES / OFFICE USE

This cannot be tested and covered in a day for new members but over several days, however they should bring this or the summary version and review each time from a senior authorized to do so. Use this master as a template answer key.

THIS CANDIDATE HAS PASSED **SAR OPERATOR CHALLENGE INITIAL** _____ **DATED** _____ **COINED? Y**

WHEN TO SWITCH TO POLO SHIRTS

The Polo Shirt usually signifies full member and one who has completed all the basics.
Once signed off on this "OTC2" standard in this document (if not before) the member can start wearing the ERT SAR Polo Shirt. It is recommended that they buy at least 2 to 3 if they expect to do overnight and consecutive day missions otherwise the one should so for now (pending availability in stores.).

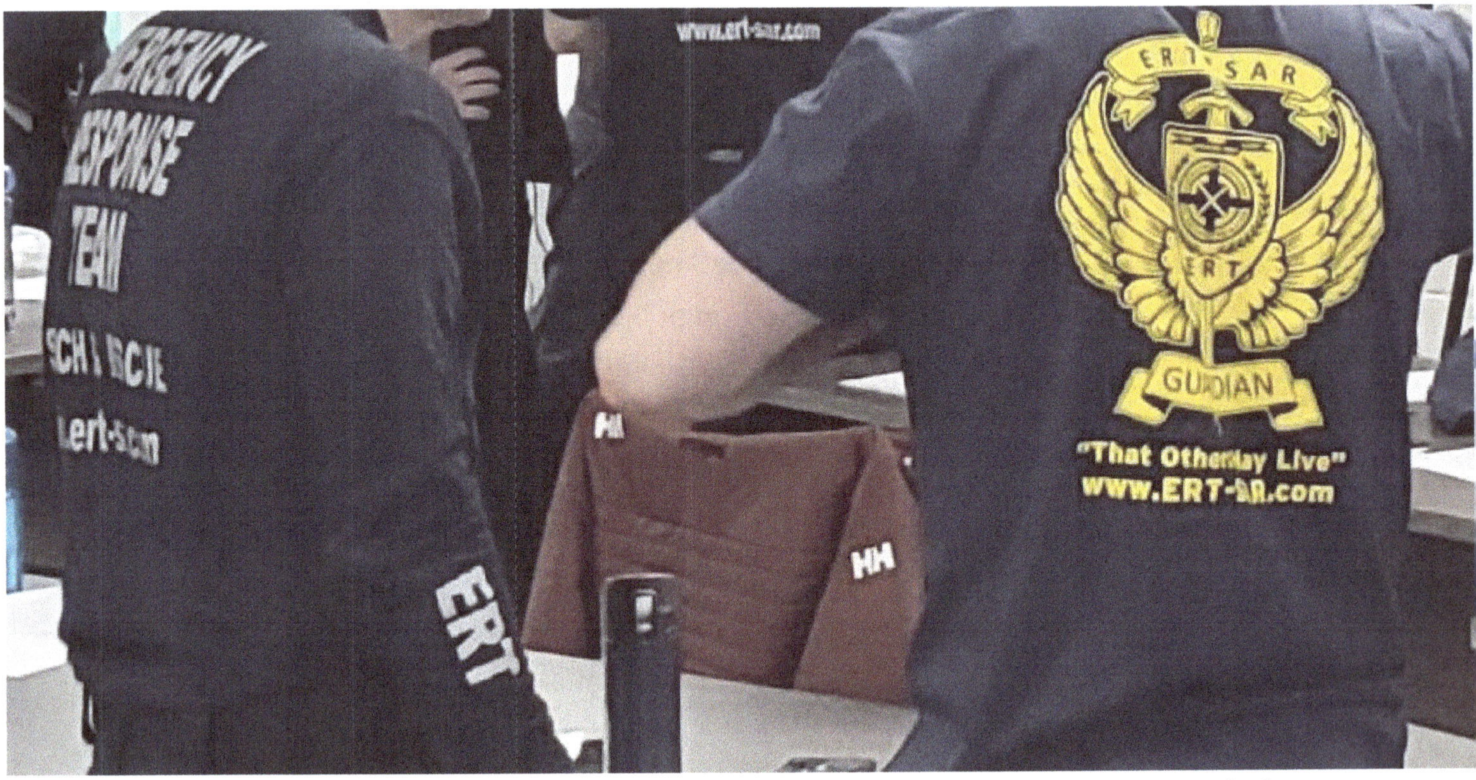

Rescuers can use this template as a guide.

Last Resort Belt / Riggers Belt can be worn by SRTs with Ops Rope and Rope Rescue Techs.

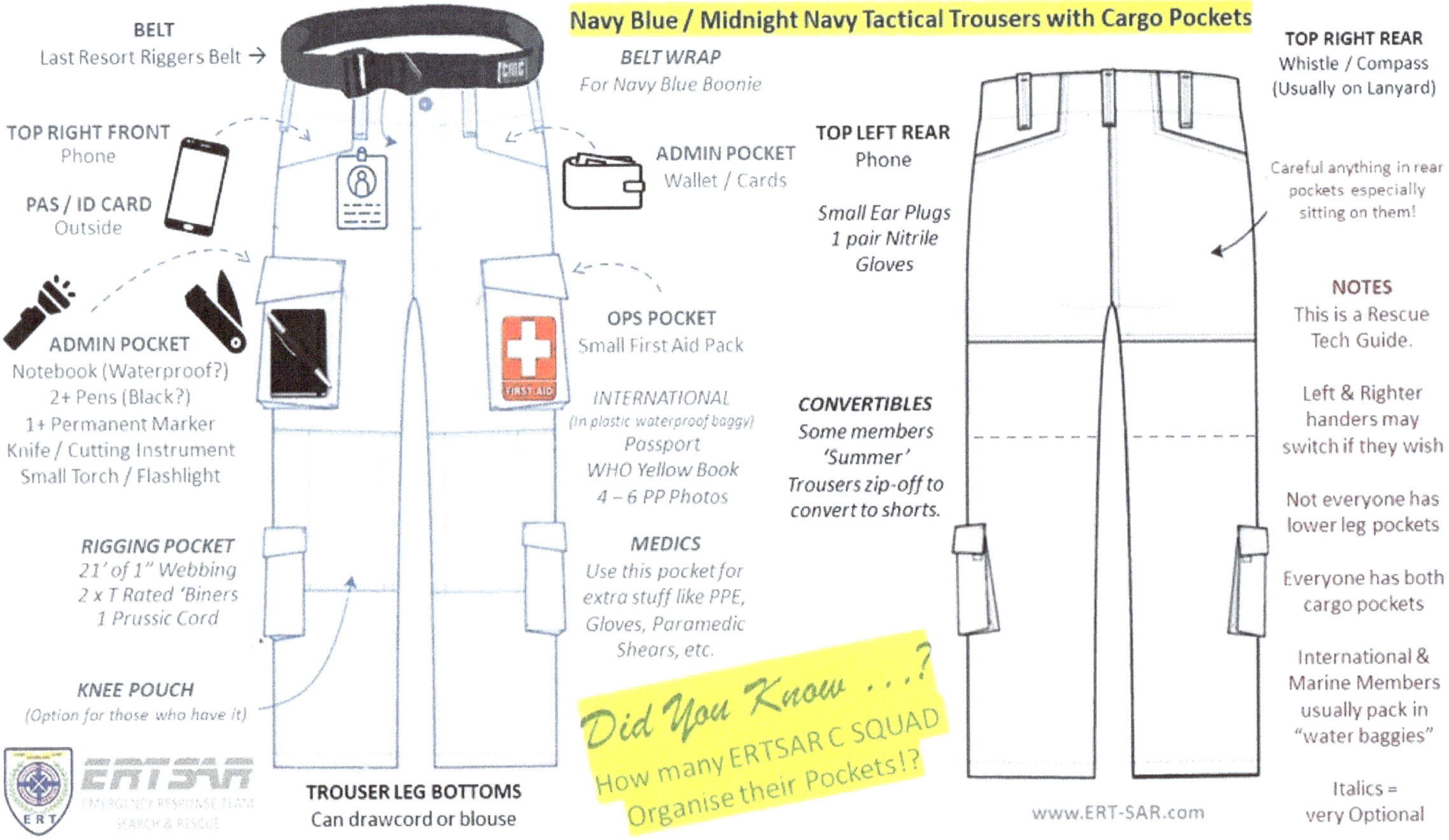